Damage Done

Author's Other Works

Glimmers of God Everywhere: Catching Sight of the Daily Divine
Six Ways to Pray from Six Great Saints
Reel Spirit Guides
Be Comforted
The Heart's Healing Journey
A Retreat with Gerard Manley Hopkins and Hildegard of Bingen: Turning Pain Into Power
A Retreat with Teresa of Avila: Living By Holy Wit
Connecting with God, Ourselves, and the People in Our Lives
Christ Encounters: A Journal Retreat
Praying the Rosary: New Reflections on the Mysteries
Praying the Way: Reflections on the Stations of the Cross
Mary and Inner Healing: An Armchair Pilgrimage to Lourdes
Jesus and John: A Story About Friends--For Friends
Created for Great Things: Spiritual Writings of Mother Teresa (editor)

Damage Done

SUICIDE OF AN ONLY SON

Gloria Hutchinson

ISBN-13: 9781496170767
ISBN-10: 1496170768
Library of Congress Control Number: 2014904596
CreateSpace Independent Publishing Platform
North Charleston, South Carolina

*This book is a memorial to
David Lorne Hutchinson,
beloved son, faithful friend.*

ACKNOWLEDGMENTS

The birth of every book is attended by midwives who makes its passage into life possible. This book is no exception. All of the following participated in the birth of *Damage Done*. Without them, this book would still be a grieving mother's aborted hope.

The three close friends who read the manuscript and responded with life-giving encouragement are: Barbara Yuodsnukis, retired reading tutor in Brunswick, ME and a long-term Hospice volunteer; Pastor Elaine Hewes of Redeemer Lutheran Church in Bangor, ME, and Valerie Osborne, consultant for the Northeastern Maine Library District, Bangor. Each of these women also offered ideas and inspirations throughout the writing process. My gratitude for their participation is unlimited.

Damage Done might never have seen the light of day without the invaluable production assistance of Marge Adams who gamely set out to compensate for my lack of computer skills. Her generosity, compassion and know-how saved me from months of incurable frustration. She volunteered her countless hours of labor as a memorial to David. We will be forever grateful to her.

I appreciate the editorial contributions of Pamela Shellberg, a professor of theology, and the church council president at Redeemer Lutheran Church, Bangor. Her insights were most helpful.

I am deeply thankful for the courageous contributions of those who shared their personal stories in Chapter 9, Seeking Peace. Jeanne and Joe Mitcho, Kathy and Ed Dyson, and Bruce Buckley openly shared their stories of lost loved ones. Others who appear in that chapter prefer that their real names not appear. I value their willingness to speak of painful memories for the benefit of others who have considered taking their own lives.

Chapter 6, Without You is enriched by the memories of Alan Yuodsnukis, Bill Gehring, and Lisa Littlefield (formerly Hutchinson). Their appreciation and assessments of our son's character enriched our own understanding of who David was to others. We will long be grateful for their generosity.

A fourth category of assistants encompasses those who contributed feedback, resources, and crucial prayer support. They include: Carole Presson (my dear sister), Elaine McGillicuddy, Janet and Dennis Boyd, Betsy and Paul Cole, Ginny Robinson, Willie Monroe, Arline and Richard Caron, Cindy McCormack, Carol Kulberg and Judith Coscarelli. Technical advice, networking and reliable support was consistently offered by our son's close friend and "brother," Bruce Nadeau, and his son Nick Levesque.

Readers will be able to hear the CD of David's song entitled *Any Day Now* (soundcloud.net) which was provided by his long-time friend Jim Roese (nhsoundeguy@aol.com) of Rochester, NH. Nor could the CD have been recorded without the talents of David's fellow musicians in the band Lester Max: Larry Ladrie, drummer; Ron Robinson, bass; and Mark Edgerly, lead guitar. We are especially grateful to these musician-friends who are helping us to honor our son.

I owe a debt of gratitude to Kirsten Hutchinson of Fairbanks, AK and Jessy Danner of Woodbridge, VA, our beloved granddaughters, for sharing their memories of David despite the emotional cost to themselves. Thanks are also due to our "Indian family," the Patels (Ken, Komal, Dinesh, Sharda, Jamini and her husband Chetan Dave) for their constant and varied assistance.

I am also thankful to Ginnie Gale and the publishing staff of CreateSpace for their professional expertise and patience with my endless questions.

Finally, my wholehearted thanks to my husband, Dave Hutchinson, for encouragement and emotional support throughout the long months of telling our son's story. This book is our way of honoring the one who was the love of our lives.

Don't kill yourself. Suffer here with
us instead.
We need you with us, we have not
forgotten you, you are our hero. Stay.

--Jennifer Michael Hecht, *On Suicide*

CONTENTS

ACKNOWLEDGMENTS   vii

INTRODUCTION   xv

CHAPTER 1

BLACK TUESDAY   1

The author recreates the morning she found her son's suicide note

CHAPTER 2

DAMAGE DONE   5

Discovering how an original rock song foreshadowed a suicide

CHAPTER 3

ONLY THE LONELY   9

A eulogy reveals damage done by inner complications

CHAPTER 4

STARRY, STARRY NIGHT   13

A memorial celebrates David's brilliance and admits his addictions

CHAPTER 5

MISSING DAD   19

Two daughters honor dad by following their bliss

CHAPTER 6
WITHOUT YOU
27

Friends validate the difference one life makes

CHAPTER 7
SOUL IMAGES
35

Searching for clues to David's suicide in the family album`

CHAPTER 8
SEEKING OBLIVION
49

An ancient wisdom source casts light on David's despair

CHAPTER 9
SEEKING PEACE
53

Sharing stories of attempted or completed suicides seeking peace

CHAPTER 10
COUNTING THE WAYS
65

David's parents count the ways they love him still

CHAPTER 11
BREAKING FAITH
71

The author's letter to David expresses anger at and forgiveness for his self-destruction

CHAPTER 12
IDENTITY CRISIS
77

How survivors cope with lost identities caused by suicide

CHAPTER 13
HOPE SECURED
83

Clues in visions, dreams, scripture that suicides "go to heaven"

CONTENTS

CHAPTER 14
SUICIDE UNSHAMED 91
Using David's story to drag suicide "out of the closet;" recognizing role of addictions and mental illness; moving beyond secrecy, shame, and judgment

CHAPTER 15
FINDING DAVID 99
Sifting evidence in a lost son's favorite movies and music to draw him closer as a singer of life

EPILOGUE 105

RESOURCES FOR CARING READERS: 107
List A Ten Signs That a Person May Be Considering Suicide
List B Ten Things You Can Do to Help the Would-Be Suicide
List C Ten Ways to Be Part of the Suicide Solution
List D Ten Songs to Comfort the Grieving
List E Ten Poems to Ease the Pain
List F Ten Books to Inform and Inspire
List G Ten Movies to Deepen Love for Life
List H Ten Scriptural Messages of Hope in Hard Times
List I The Author's Advice from Hard Experience

A PRAYER FOR THOSE WHO ARE DECIDING NOT TO GO ON 121

INTRODUCTION

*If a man does not keep pace with his
companions, perhaps it is because he
hears a different drummer. Let him
step to the music he hears, however
measured or far away.*

Henry David Thoreau

Our son is dead. He was an only son, an only child, a lonely child. David's pain ended on the night of Nov. 5, 2012 when he shot himself in the heart. Our pain began on the morning after when I found the cryptic note he left on the table at the foot of his empty bed.

"I am in the woods across the road."

Next to the note was a copy of his will, a will we had no idea existed because he was not one to attend to unnecessary details nor was he given to long-range planning. He left everything he owned to his eldest daughter Kirsten.

There were no other notes, no apologies or explanations. He hated emotional demonstrations which he called soap operas or dramas.

Our pain lies like a stone on our worn hearts. Its weight varies from day to day but is never completely lifted. The choice our son made freed him from an unendurable burden. It laid on us a task for which we were miserably unprepared.

We had to learn to live, to drag ourselves out of bed every day, knowing that we would be deprived of hearing our son's familiar voice, of seeing his appealing face, of counting on his physical presence for the rest of our lives.

The possibility of his ever actually taking his own life had never penetrated the parental armor in which our hearts were wrapped. No matter how depressed he became, he would never "do that" to us, to his daughters, to his extended family and friends. We never dared to look behind his mask to confront the terror of his self-destruction.

The note that Tuesday morning was a death knell to the former selves we who loved him had been. For his father and me, it was the ultimate identity theft. No more "Dad." No "Mom." Now we were just Dave and Gloria. The three had become two. And two suddenly seemed "the loneliest number."

Those who are left standing after the suicide of a loved one are called *survivors*. Our primary task is to figure out how to go on living after the terminally disorienting death of a child, spouse or cherished friend by his or her own hand. Some of us succeed. Others do not.

One estimate suggests that a survivor's chances of committing suicide increase by 400 per cent. Like us, all survivors need to be kind to themselves and tend to their psychological-spiritual health. *Damage Done* is intended to be a source of guidance for them, as well as for others who are among the estimated one million Americans attempting suicide each year.

This book is also the author's way of staying alive and arguably sane. By telling our son's story, I hope to give some meaning to his self-inflicted death, some companionship to other survivors who are walking this same hard road, and some guidance to good-hearted readers who wonder how they can help prevent suicide.

Most importantly, *Damage Done* is a memorial to David who sought so long and hard for his place in life, his peace of mind, his conviction of belonging. Like so many other rock n' roll musicians, he got derailed by the addictions of that late-night-on-the-road lifestyle. His story will ring true to anyone who has sampled that same life. He would want his story to be a cautionary tale to deter others from the self-destruction that claimed him.

David tried to live by Joseph Campbell's dictum: "Follow your bliss and the universe will open doors for you where there were only walls." He did know bliss. But the doors he needed most remained locked.

As I write these words, months have gone by since that morning, the morning he did not appear for his cigarette on the back deck and his coffee in the living room. That morning he was scheduled to appear in court for an offense that would most likely have merited a fine and a required attendance at AA meetings. That morning he did not respond when I called him.

That morning it never crossed my mind that my son did not answer because he, who had been so calm and content in recent weeks, had already put an end to his 48 years on this earth.

Our son is dead. We are not ourselves.

CHAPTER 1

BLACK TUESDAY

Everyone is a moon, and has a dark side
which he never shows to anybody.

--Mark Twain

Terror dazed me. I could not think what to do. Like a dumb animal attempting to evade a predator, I plodded down the stairs to David's rooms. In the dim light, I could not see if he was in his bed. The pile of pillows could have been a sleeping person. But they were simply their mute selves. And the bed was uncreased, unoccupied.

Gasping, I ran up the stairs, somehow certain that I would find him in the back yard or in the garage. These certainties were nonsensical but reason had fled. "David!," I called repeatedly. "David!"

I rushed back down the stairs. There I saw, for the first time, the note and the will on the table at the foot of his bed. "Jesus!," I shouted. It was my life's most fervent prayer.

Jesus did not appear. But he helped me dial 911 and clearly tell the dispatcher that my son was missing, he had left a note, and here is our address in Bangor. "The police are on their way," she replied, in that emotion-free tone intended to calm the caller.

I knew I had to call my husband in Florida and let him know. He had driven our motorhome south a few weeks earlier to set up for the winter season. How could Dave bear to hear this news when he was so far from home, and when he had stifled some dark intuitions about David's possible depression?

"I'm on my way," he assured me. I can't recall what else he said. Memory has drawn the curtain on much of what went on that black Tuesday in November. Our driveway filled up with black and white cruisers. Brian Strout, a state police detective who lives next door, came over to consult with the searchers and offer comfort.

My first responder-friends, Carol and Judith, dispensed hugs, bottles of water, and soothing reminders that we did not yet know what David had done after he wrote the note.

"I am in the woods across the road."

Maybe he had gone into the woods and simply kept walking out the other side. Thousands of people every day plan to kill themselves. But they change their minds. Maybe he had changed his mind. My friends believed in that possibility. My gut did not.

Pastor Elaine Hewes came through the door and immediately embraced me in a sheltering hug. Other friends and neighbors gathered in the living room in an attempt to create a human shield against the threat of tragedy. I was surrounded by compassionate people who could do nothing to spare me from being alone in the most profound way.

"They've found him," Brian said, striding through the front door with a look that said all I did not want to hear.

They had located David's body deep in the woods. He had shot himself through the heart.

My own heart hurt as though someone had punched me in the chest. I remember screaming, "No! No!," and "What a waste! What a waste!"

Our beautiful, talented, good-hearted son had ended his life in midstream. He would never again walk through the door, saying "Hey, Dad" or "Hi Mom." I erupted into explosive rounds of "I can't bear it, I can't bear it!"

Elaine held me firmly as I sobbed, "I'm so angry, Elaine!" She stroked my hair and said, "Of course you are. You have every right to be angry. Go ahead and let it out."

Someone handed me a throw pillow and I hurled it at the nearest wall, once again shouting, "What a waste!" The witnesses who knew me as a calm religious person must have been horrified. They could not have known that my anger was aimed at myself for not having discerned the sign's of David's desperation.

Pastor Elaine called us all into a prayer circle: friends, policemen, neighbors of varied faiths and levels of belief. Speaking as bluntly as a football coach on the eve of a championship game, she said, "Before we pray together, I want to make sure that no one in this circle believes the 'B.S.' the church formerly taught about those who take their own lives. God is love and David is with God."

David is with God. David is with God. God, I do believe. Help my unbelief!

Thankfully, I would not know until later that on the way home from Florida, Dave's car had been struck by a large deer. The car was totaled. Dave was unharmed. The tow truck driver who took him to a motel confided that his own son had died two months earlier. "I took him to the hospital because he had a bad pain in his stomach and he died that same night," the driver said. "It's rough. You won't get over it any time soon."

When Dave's brother Richard and son Jean Paul came from Maine to pick him up in Pennsylvania, the troubles were not yet over. They encountered a blizzard in Connecticut that stuck with them throughout New England. By the time Dave and I finally wrapped our arms around each other it was 4:30 a.m.

Too exhausted to sleep, too devastated to care, we lay staring at the ceiling.

It was, for us, the day the music died.

CHAPTER 2

DAMAGE DONE

*He took his pain and turned it into
something beautiful. Into something
that people connect to. And that's what
good music does. It speaks to you. It
changes you.*

--Hannah Harrington

David was a rock musician, composer and self-taught sound engineer. He lived in his head, stockpiling his emotions in a cavern marked "Keep out." As his friend Bruce observed, "He kept his feelings to himself. Even his wives and daughters never knew what was really going on with him."

Although he hid his true self, David's music sometimes betrayed him. It held a mirror to his soul. It carried him past the walls he set up between him and self-revelation. It disclosed the truth to those who could bear it. We were not among them.

One of the last songs he wrote is perhaps the most confessional. His friend Jim Roese, a professional sound engineer, recorded *Any Day*

Now after David's death. Although David had recorded it himself several times, he was never satisfied with the results. His characteristic insistence on perfection robbed him of the joy of launching this song on a CD or the internet.

Although I had heard an early version of *Any Day Now*, I got carried away with the upbeat music while the lyrics mostly escaped me. My hearing loss and his poor quality microphone combined to cloud the words. I guessed that the lyrics might have recalled a previous time in his life when alcoholism had derailed him. I had no idea that they were prophetic.

Why was I so dense? Was it because our son was such a consummate actor that I thought he was pleased with his creation and I was pleased for him? God Almighty, why didn't I suspect the truth that now seems conspicuous?

Perhaps it was because human beings "cannot bear very much reality" (T. S. Eliot). Our fear of losing someone is commensurate with our love for them. Anyone who has ever survived a suicide needs no further explanation.

Any Day Now
(David Hutchinson)

Ooooh, any day now
Find myself unchained
From ghosts of simple lovin' souls I've stained.

Mmmmmm, any day now
Innocent again
And free to let the good old days begin.

No more dues, no more addiction,
Sick of blues and self-inflicted haze.
See the unseen stash of endless

Things I'm sure could mend my mendless days
Mmmmm, with unclouded gaze.

Ooooh, any day now
I'll find a simple way
To keep the flood of bad ideas at bay.

I've taken roads wouldn't recommend,
Countless short-cuts to the bitter end.
I've taken all, I've been taken in
And taken down by fun I warmeth in
And did it all again. . .but ran away.

Ooooh, any day now
I'll put away the gun
Use to shoot the messengers that come.

Ooooh, any day now
I'll make peace with the sun
For always showing up when rain is done,
For always showing up when rain is done. . .

Mmmmm, damage done.

[copyright 2013]

(You can hear the recording of David's song made by Jim Roese (nh-soundguy@aol.com) on soundcloud.com.)

The first time Dave and I heard this recording after our son's suicide, with the lyrics loud and clear, we were torn apart by hearing him yet no longer having him.

Damage done.

The original Lester Max band (l to r): Jim Roese, Larrdy Ladrie, and David Hutchinson.

CHAPTER 3

ONLY THE LONELY

Loneliness is the first thing which
God's eye named not good.

--John Milton

In the first several months after David's self-inflicted death, my stock of retrievable memories focused unrelentingly on his aloneness. During the weeks before his death, several of those closest to him failed to respond to his crucial need for connection. They (and we) were engrossed in other concerns, and did not sense a tragedy brewing.

Throughout his life, David's needs for connection and solitude were at war in his soul. When he had one, he needed the other. Although he was married three times, he was single for the last few years of his life. His closest friend and band mate, Bruce Nadeau, focused on this theme in his eulogy at David's memorial service.

"If there was one thing David was not good at--it was relationships. I mean, how do you have three marriages and only two wives?," Bruce observed. Commending David's second wife Lisa for trying so hard to make it work, Bruce added, "Fifteen years of marriage off and on. I be-lieve you were soul mates who just couldn't get along."

Knowing that David himself would have scoffed at any attempt to sanctify him, Bruce continued: "David was hard to get along with. He was very strong willed and opinionated at times. If you disagreed with what he thought, you were going to get an earful. It was much easier at times to say "ah-huh" and "yeah" than to argue with him."

Bruce went on to note how David's problems in connecting with oth-ers denied him the joy of having contented relationships with his two daughters. "To what extent he deserved what happened really doesn't matter now. You can't change the past."

Addressing Kirsten and Jessy in the front row, he added, "I just want you to know that although your dad was not perfect, he loved you both dearly and would have liked nothing better than to have a normal father-daughter relationship throughout your whole lives."

Looking directly at the young women whose father was his best friend, Bruce commented, "But he was a complicated man."

Those complications included a tendency to over-analyze others' mo-tivations.. "He would sometimes change what you said into something completely different. He didn't mean to. But a person can't help the way they think. This habit put David at a disadvantage. For all the wonderful, thoughtful, insightful things he did for all of us, if you can't help look-ing for deeper meanings, and there aren't any, it's bound to cause riffs in relationships."

Bruce then turned to what he described as "the only relationship in David's life that was always constant." Dave and I braced ourselves. But we had nothing to dread. We heard ourselves lauded for supporting David in every endeavor, appreciating his talents, always being there for him in troubled times.

"Young Dave loved his father. And Big Dave certainly loved his son. Being men, father and son share a certain kind of bond. But the bond a mother shares with her son is special. Gloria and David had that special bond. And I know this was only strengthened by the quality time they spent together these last few weeks as they laughed together, watched old movies and just really enjoyed each other's company."

My throat ached with unuttered sobs at hearing all of these truths about our only, our lonely son.

David was a complicated man.

CHAPTER 4

STARRY, STARRY NIGHT

We have always wanted something
beyond what we have wanted.

--Ernesto Cardenal

When the pastor stood to give her pastoral address at our son's memorial, few of those gathered in the chapel had any idea that they were about to hear a masterful preacher.

Most of David's friends were "unchurched," as that graceless saying has it. But from her opening lines, Elaine Hewes drew us all into the depth of her regard for him whom she had never met--except in his music and in the shared memories of his loved ones.

She had listened to his CD *Not Roger* (performed by the group Lester Max) ten times, often as she tooled around town in her silver Prius "playing air guitar." Although as a classical violinist, she was not normally into rock-n-roll, she "knew brilliance" when she heard it.

Commending our son's music, she wondered how the album could have been anything other than brilliant when it was the product of

"David's work, David's efforts, David's passion, David's demons, David's energy, David's love, David's longing."

She had come to learn of David that "he was brilliant, and he was beautiful, and he was passionate; three human characteristics which often make it challenging to live in this world." That description put her in mind of Don Maclean's song *Vincent* which he wrote in tribute to Vincent van Gogh.

The lyrics refer to that "starry, starry night" (the title of one of the artist's best known works) when "you took your life, as lovers often do." Van Gogh's depressions and financial dependence on his brother Theo finally brought him to despair. David's depressions, relationship failures and addiction to alcohol led him to the same spiritual blackout. As Maclean puts it, "This world was never meant/For one as beautiful as you."

Recognizing how deeply his fellow musicians and his family loved him, the pastor enumerated some of their favorite David-things: blueberry everything and Mountain Dew; classic guitars and collectible seashells; movies like *The Jerk* and his spot-on imitation of Steve Martin's "All I need is this" routine; the way David invested his artistic abilities in jazzing up the family convenience store and turning his apartment into a haven for unusual houseplants and whimsical decor (a life-sized Betty Boop, a five-foot knight in shining armor, a polka-dotted fish sporting crimson lipstick).

Then Pastor Elaine turned to the one image of David that she felt "speaks to the depth of his heart from the time he was just a little boy." She read from the book I had written and our son had produced: *Glimmers of God Everywhere: Catching Sight of the Daily Divine*. The epigraph to the chapter about young David is a gospel verse: "What can one give in exchange for his life?" (Mt 16:26).

The story in my book recounts how I took five-year old David with me to a Catholic bookstore and invited him to choose whichever book he liked. He gave serious attention to his task, picking up one and then another glossy covered children's volume. Eventually he held up *Life of Jesus for Little People*. He wondered what it was about.

"It's all about Jesus and it tells you how to save your life," I said.

"Really? How much is it?"

"Seventy-nine cents."

"Are you sure?"

"Yes. Why?"

"Because the price of a life hasn't even been told yet."

Without further consideration, our son informed me, "I'll take this one." And he strode toward the check-out counter.

The pastor paused at the story's end. She then pointed out that it would be false to imply that everything about David was beautiful. Like all of us, he was plagued at various times by demons of one kind or another. She listed "the demons of fear, of anger, of insecurity, of loss, of depression, anxiety, guilt."

"And in our attempts to mask the pain of these things," she continued, "we can get caught in all sorts of other things that cause us only more pain: like alcohol abuse, withdrawal from important relationships, self-defeating behaviors. David was not immune from these things. Because in one form or another, none of us are."

In retrospect, I marvel at the manner in which Elaine Hewes was able to acknowledge David's failings while reminding her listeners that each one of us tries to deaden our pain with addiction to something. While one may turn to prescription drugs or pornography, another may be consumed by the need to be richer or more righteous than his neighbor.

We are all utterly dependent on a flagrantly forgiving God.

Identifying with her listeners, the preacher noted the unanswered questions that devastate the survivors of a loved one who has taken his own life. "Why did he do it? Why didn't I do this or that? What if I had said or done something? Where the hell is God, anyway?"

She assured us that God is here among us, as surely as God was "with David every day of his life; with David on the starry, starry night of his death; with David now in completeness and a fullness that we can't begin to imagine." (Hearing this, Dave and I looked at each other through our tears, trying to smile but cramped by our need to stifle any outright crying.)

The pastor urged us to remember that "God is with us in our joy and in our suffering, in our falling and our rising, in our living and in our dying, in every moment we climb the highest mountain trying to find what we're looking for. . .in every moment we fail to find what we're looking for." (Here she was culling from David's favorite U2 song which he often performed with an intensity that deeply affected his audience: *Still Haven't Found What I'm Looking For.* The congregation was invited to sing it along with his musician friends at the memorial.)

Quoting the psalmist, the pastor continued: "Where can I go from your spirit?. . .If I climb up to heaven you are there. If I make the grave my bed you are there also (139:7-8). Although God's presence is at times like this, hard to see, "I see it today in the ways in which you gather to remember David and to comfort one another. Sometimes this is the strongest glimpse we have of the God who is love."

After urging us to keep comforting one another, the pastor called us to "The love that accompanied David through the last boundary we know as death, and has welcomed him with open arms into that place where David has finally found what he was looking for all along. . .That place where there is a sense of wholeness and peace."

However, this eloquent Lutheran pastor was not referring to some sweet abode of pink-winged cherubs or celestial choirs robed in gold. Every musician in the chapel sat up and took notice when she said: "The kind of peace that comes when the guitars are perfectly tuned with one another, and the reverb is set just right, and the drums are tight, and the lead guitar is wailing, and the vocals are blending, and the band isn't just playing the music, but the band *is* the music. . .The band *is* the music. . .Just as we who loved David will be the music now, as in thanksgiving for the one who taught us how, we sing together *Let It Be.*

At this poignant moment, David's long-time friend and fellow guitarist Dennis Boyd picked up his acoustic guitar and led us in singing that very Beatles' classic. It begins with the telling lines: *When I find myself in times of trouble,/Mother Mary comes to me."*

The singer calls on Mary as the maternal source of wisdom from whom an answer will come. Let it be.

We had those words inscribed on David's memorial card.

In the commendation, Elaine Hewes called on Jesus to acknowledge David as "a sheep of your own fold, a lamb of your own flock, a sinner of your own redeeming." She then said that the closing song we had selected earlier, *Be Not Afraid*, no longer seemed right for David. It was "too churchy."

She decided instead to sing for us, in her clarion soprano voice so like David's daughter Kirsten's, a "little song made famous by one of the great performers of our time, Kermit the Frog." It begins, "It's in every one of us to be wise./Find your heart, open up both your eyes." I thought of how wise David was in so many ways. Only he knows if his search for the Spirit was derailed by those spirits in the bottle that dragged him away from his true self.

After we had been blessed by the pastor, and blessed again by hearing David's endearing voice singing *Any Day Now*, Elaine Hewes gave us her last word.

"In thanksgiving for the life of David, let us go and *be* the music."

Let it be.

CHAPTER 5

MISSING DAD

It doesn't matter who my father was;
it matters who I remember he was.

--Anne Sexton

They do not call each other step-sisters. They are sisters with separate mothers. Kirsten Hutchinson, 24, and Jessica (Jessy), Danner, 22, are united by their strong resemblances to their father. They are bound for life by their memories of the man they call "dad."

He was often missing from their lives, rarely by his own choice. He appreciated their mothers' crucial roles in their upbringing and never tried to wrest them away. Even when stepfathers entered the picture, David willingly took a back seat in order to avoid any conflict that would cause his daughters harm. In retrospect, Kirsten and Jessy wish that he had been more assertive in gaining a larger presence in their lives. But, as adults, they know that he could not take that approach. His conviction of his own unworthiness stopped him.

"There were times when we did not get along and didn't even speak," Kirsten says. "I used to get upset when he didn't call me regularly. Eventually I learned that that was just the way he was. It didn't mean that he didn't love me. I came to accept him for who he was and to focus on what I loved about him. This is one of the most important lessons I've learned in my life so far."

Kirsten cherishes the ways in which hers and her father's personalities mirrored each other. "I love that we agreed on so many things we talked about. I love that we have a whole history of memories together. I love how he seemed to disappear into the music whenever he was playing guitar." Referring to her own career in music, she says she tries to follow David's example whenever she is stressed out about her vocal recitals or operatic performances.

She loves the way in which her dad was always on a quest for knowledge and understanding of what truly matters in life. "He lived passionately, and I try to do the same. He wanted me to push as hard as I could to pursue my music and develop my talent. He wanted me to search and explore like he did in Los Angeles. But, most of all, he just wanted me to sing."

Kirsten recalls that she and her father often spoke about relationships, more hers than his. However, she believes that the same truths apply whether for daughter or father. "It is hard to be passionate and not to receive the same passion in return," she says. "And it is difficult to feel understood. When you don't have that assurance, especially about the ones you love most, it's very easy to feel alone--which makes you want to protect yourself. I fight that feeling often in relationships, and maybe my dad did too."

David's eldest daughter feels that they both shared a talent for listening to others, analyzing what they heard, and giving advice that was "well thought out and well worded." She laughs over their matching "easygoing attitudes about what activities we should participate in. It was horrible when it was just the two of us. We could never decide what to do! We always ended up taking walks, watching movies, or just talking together. It mattered more who we were with."

Their close kinship, she feels, is verified in her dad's and her psychological pattern of being intensely social at times and deeply introverted at others. Like her father, she withdraws from conflict and needs time alone to sort out whatever decisions need to be made.

Among her happy memories of her father is hearing him tell the story of his and Lisa's honeymoon in Jamaica. "He made it sound so wonderful that I have decided if I ever have a honeymoon, that's where I want to go." She delights in her father's having named his and Lisa's dog "Bob" and their cat "Marley." And she holds sweet memories of ice skating with David on the family's pond in Carthage, ME where "My dad was never afraid to be silly just for me."

Kirsten regrets that her father may have thought that she no longer needed him even though she is certain of the opposite. She regrets that he will not be there to walk her down the aisle when she eventually weds. She is sorry that the two of them will never get to go parasailing as they planned. She rues the reality that he will not be there to cheer her on as she advances in her music career.

"And I am sad that he will not be here to know the children I may have. Since my grandparents played such important roles in my life, I hate to think of his missing out on spoiling his grandchildren. He would have been very good at that."

At the time of David's suicide, Kirsten found it odd that so few friends and acquaintances expressed their sympathies. "I guess they didn't know what to say. It's not the same as having your parent die of cancer. I will never know why he did it. I think he did not want me to know why."

David's younger daughter Jessy recalls that she was at drama school in London when Kirsten called her to tell her of their father's death. "It was the only time in my life that I have felt emotion like that. It was terrifying. I had only cried maybe once in the five previous years. So I didn't have any clue how to deal with his suicide. I ran outside and attempted to light a cigarette. All I could think of was, 'I should have sent that [blankety-blank] e-mail!'"

She and David had been separated for several years for reasons neither was clear about and which both misunderstood. Through Kirsten's intercession, Jessy had agreed to meet her sister in Paris for a reunion. Their talks about David allowed her to see him as he truly was. They also awakened her to what she had been missing.

"Kirsten shared with me a story about one of the recent times when they had been together and, in a candid moment, he told her how much he loved her and how proud he was of her. I realized I wanted a moment like that. I wanted to hear my dad say those things. I wanted my father in my life. I decided to send him an e-mail as soon as I figured out exactly what I wanted to say. I wrote it but I wasn't satisfied with it. This was a week before his death."

Jessy recalls how incredibly angry she was at herself for not sending that e-mail. "Even if it wouldn't have changed anything, even if it made him angry, even if he wanted nothing to do with me, he could have known how I missed him. That is one thing I'll always regret--that I'll never get a chance to tell him that I love him, that I miss him, and that I'm so overwhelmingly sorry it took me so long to realize it."

What Jessy did not know or expect was that when Kirsten told their father that she and Jessy were to be reunited in Paris, he was so overcome with happiness at the prospect that he cried. He was sure that once they met as adults, they would never be estranged again. And had he been alive to receive his youngest daughter's letter, anger and rejection would have been the furthest things from his mind.

Jessy had no idea that her dad had continued to display her portraits from childhood and early teens throughout his apartment, and that he boasted to friends about her budding career as an actress-singer-model which he tracked on Facebook. He held no grudges against her for choosing to opt out of his life. She was his daughter and he had never ceased to love her.

Because she has had her own past problems with addiction and relationships, Jessy now has a deeper understanding of her father's difficulties with wives, partners, and daughters.

"I think it goes back to living too much in his head. When you spend so much time with your thoughts, dealing with other people can be a challenge. You get so focused on analyzing every thing and everyone around you, including yourself, that relationships can be very difficult to maintain. I know that my dad had people around him who loved and cared for him. But sometimes it is hard to accept that. You kind of build a wall around yourself and then wonder why you feel so alone--even when you are the one keeping a distance."

Jessy sees some important similarities with her father. "We both love music, and I think we book took as much, if not more, joy in the creation and process of art than in the actual performance. Since we're both so introverted, performance itself is a huge outlet for us. In fact, it's the only time I'm comfortable 'letting people in.' From what I've heard, my dad was the same way."

She notes that both of them had problems with addiction which were related to their introversion. "I know when I was younger, I struggled for years with severe depression and suicidal tendencies, and that definitely fueled my drug addiction, and vice versa."

Wanting to avoid further reflection on her father's death, Jessy switches to a clear memory she treasures, a memory of a time when she and David were in harmony. Her dad wanted to buy Jessy her first guitar.

"He took me to a music store and chatted with the owner while I looked around. My first choice was the cheapest one they had--a shiny black one with a decal of claw marks on the side. Hey, I was twelve! I was easily seduced by aesthetics. When I showed it to him, he told me that I could do way better than that, and pointed me to the Fenders."

She smiles at the memory of her father's delight in teaching her what a quality guitar looked like. "A matte purple Stratocaster immediately caught my eye, and I fell in love. I think we were both pretty happy with the decision--him because it was a genuinely good instrument, and me because it looked so cool. I remember that we were both very proud that day. It's still my favorite guitar and the only one I've ever played at a gig."

Jessy and Kirsten are mourning their missing dad in different ways. Jessy is "forcing emotions down and not dealing with them" while keeping extremely busy. She hasn't allowed herself to contemplate David's suicide "partly because I have no idea how and partly because I'm scared to even try." However, her dad's death has assured her "That all those emotions are there."

Kirsten tries to face her feelings of bereavement and turns to her partner Will for consolation. "My father's death makes me so very sad, and I know it always will. It is never going to change. I do believe that I have be O.K. with it."

With a maturity born of sadness, Kirsten says, "I know that whatever my father dealt with and whatever made him do what he did was much bigger than me. My dad told me that he wanted me to do big things with my life, so I'm trying my absolute best to do that--for both of us."

David's daughters are honoring him by striving to follow their bliss into lifetime careers in music and acting. By doing so, they may well turn their mourning into joy.

What more could any father ask?

CHAPTER 6

WITHOUT YOU

You have to live not only for yourself,
but for the precious person in your
life who has died--to work on his
unfinished work and to realize his
unfinished dreams.

--Alan D. Wolfelt

One great consolation for us has been hearing the stories of friends in whose lives David made a lasting difference. The second-class angel in Frank Capra's *It's a Wonderful Life* persuades the suicidal George Bailey to recognize how his presence in Bedford Falls has helped others. Once George sees the light, the angel observes, "Strange, isn't it? Each man's life touches so many other lives. When he isn't around he leaves an awful hole, doesn't he?"

If David and every other suicide had been given the opportunity to hear witnesses like the ones that follow, would that have been enough to at least give them pause? I do not pretend to know the answer. I only know that hearing these witnesses' stories draws us closer to our missing son.

1. A Boyhood Idol

In a four-page handwritten letter sent to Dave and me, Alan Yuodsnukis recalls the first time he met David. Alan was a second grader and David was four grades ahead of him. Religion classes at St. Charles Church in Brunswick, ME had just finished, when Alan heard a thumping noise down the hall.

When he went to investigate, he found David hurling erasers at a target drawn on the blackboard. Alan writes, "He hit the bull's eye every time, and without batting an eye, he tossed me an eraser and said, 'Wanna play?' Big kids just didn't do that with little kids. My older brother and his friends would have told me to get lost. Even at that age, David had that extremely rare combination of cool and kindness."

Alan recalls watching David in high school playing basketball and guitar, both skills he wanted to emulate. Carefully observing David performing with his guitar, the younger boy saw something more than talent on display. "I can only call it grace. It brought him great joy, as it did to us who were listening."

Both Alan and his brother Joel would later receive free guitar lessons from David. They stuck with it for awhile but then moved on to other pursuits that did not require as much practice. However, they had no doubt that David had been born to make music.

The last time Alan encountered David in person was at his wedding reception in Fort Kent, ME where the bridegroom's band played long into the night. "To me he will always be that same happy young man who kept us smiling, rocking and dancing until he got to go home with the prettiest girl in the room (Deena Dubois). He was the guy I wanted to be, even from the first time I met him."

Alan went on to say: "As David had his music and his sound studio, I have fly fishing and rivers. It is my passion and they are my chapel." He observed that his favorite book, Norman Maclean's *A River Runs Through It*, is not only a celebration of fly fishing but a memoir honoring the author's younger brother Paul "who had prodigious talents but fought a losing battle with personal demons that ended with his murder."

That last line hooked me into reading *A River Runs Through It* despite my complete disinterest in fly fishing. Alan implied that there were resemblances between Paul Maclean and David. He had also quoted extensively from the book because he recognized the author's deep-water wisdom.

I discovered that Paul Maclean was a genius at the art of fly fishing which bound him, his brother and his father (a retired minister) together. His father describes him with one word: "Beautiful." Norman regrets how little he knows his brother, and how Paul "looks to himself" for help when he is in trouble.

His family refrains from nagging Paul about his heavy drinking, promiscuous women and high stakes gambling. They do not really want to know the extent of his self-destructive habits. They treasure his artistry with the fly fishing rod and his characteristic thoughtfulness towards them. They do not want to imperil their relationship with him.

As Norman says, "You can love completely without complete understanding" (p. 103).

After Paul's savagely beaten body is found in an alley, the apparent victim of mobsters taking revenge for unpaid gambling debts, his father observes, "It is those we live with and love and should know who elude us" (p. 104).

Finally, if I still had any doubts that Paul Maclean and our son were cut from the same dark cloth, I read that Paul's mother never asked any questions about the things that led to his tragic death, an indirect suicide caused by choosing a dark path.

"Perhaps she knew enough to know that for her it was enough to have loved him," Norman observes (p. 102).

Thanks to a young friend who had chosen David as his boyhood idol, I found in *A River Runs Through It* the companionship of a family that had suffered a loss like ours with as little understanding of the one who left them.

2. A Dedicated Teacher

His band mates called him "Mr. Bill" in an affectionate allusion to the clay character who debuted on *Saturday Night Live* in 1976. Bill Gehring was a classroom teacher in Northern Maine when he first met David in 1985. Together with the drummer Bruce Nadeau, they became Bruce and the Crewcuts, and later The Checkers.

"I remember my first impression of him was, "This is one talented guy. What's he doing in Fort Kent? I had been playing with a bunch of guys who weren't all that good. Thank God, Dave got me out of that. Then later when we collaborated on a few songs--80% vs. 20%, with me as the 20%--I was thinking 'Lennon-McCartney', you know? Dave really changed my life--and not just in music."

(To his friends David was always 'Dave.' But within the family, he was 'David' in order to avoid winding up as the dreaded 'Junior.')

Mr. Bill recalls how easy Dave was to talk with. "He was good at real conversation, and he was always looking for answers to important questions, always reaching for more. Even though he was younger than me, I looked up o him and respected him--music or no music. We were really connected."

Dave's roles in the bands he formed included teacher and innovator, lead guitarist and lead vocals. Bill recalls some of The Checkers' signature moves as suggested by Dave: wearing loud colored suits, sponsoring a "Spam Dance" with a can of spam as the prize, having the drummer stand, choreographing cool dance moves, adding a stand-up bass and horns to the band, doing a Blues Brothers imitation in dark glasses and trench coats, adding chandeliers and antique lamps to the stage lighting. "He was one imaginative guy," Bill recalls.

Whether the band was doing cover tunes or Dave's original music, Bruce and Mr. Bill took their lead from Dave. "He taught us, pushed us beyond what we thought we could do. He expected commitment. He set goals and we'd meet them. He was always patient with me. Made me feel that it was O.K. to make a mistake. I'm not sure if it was Dave or Mike E

C (Mike Charette, part-time front man and horn player) who started the group habit of saying 'Love you, man.' We were joking--but we meant it too."

Mr. Bill expresses his sadness that David's attempt to form a band in Los Angeles was short-lived. "He met a lot of cool musicians and played with some of them. But it didn't last." (David's explanation was that he could not bear the LA lifestyle in which his fellow musicians "never kept their word or showed up when they said they would." The contrast with his own commitment to the music was too much for him).

"He did get to tour with Bill Haley's Comets and play back-up for Tiny Tim," Mr. Bill adds. "But I just wish we could have played on a larger scale than Maine and New England. He had the talent for it."

A deeper source of sadness for Bill is the break with Dave that followed Bill's becoming a member of the Assembly of God Church.

"How do I talk to you now?," Dave wondered.

"I'm still Bill. Just talk to me like you always have."

But Dave felt that something irrevocable had come between him and Mr. Bill. "We had been so close. Instead there was a disconnect. He was living the rock n' roll life. You know, boys will be boys, drinking and partying. For awhile he switched to O'Douls (non-alcoholic beer) and tried to control his drinking. But then he went back to it. When the rest of us were ready to leave after a gig, he would stay on with other musicians and bar owners. But he never really talked seriously to me again. He was not going to let me in."

When, at one point years ago, Dave asked Mr. Bill to borrow his .22 rifle, Bill did not know, nor did we, that Dave had mentioned the possibility of shooting himself to another friend. He returned the gun without incident and Bill immediately took the gun to a pawn shop and sold it.

"Dave helped me to be a better person and a better musician. He showed me how to think my way through things and encouraged me to get out and do something with my life. The only thing was--he was good at hiding."

3. A Complicated Husband

Lisa Gagnon met David at a Thanksgiving gig in Presque Isle, ME in 1991. He was fascinated by her brilliant blue eyes and good-time smile. She was irresistibly attracted by his musical talents and "soulful stage presence."

That very first night he told her that he had two daughters and a failed marriage to one of their mothers. He also assured her that she was going to be "the future Mrs. Hutchinson," and that they had been brought together for a purpose.

Looking back a few months after David's suicide, Lisa wrote: "Evidence early on showed that he was a very sensitive, deeply insecure person with major trust issues. It was also evident that he was extremely intelligent and introspective. I had no idea how difficult life would be with him."

Lisa discerned in David's original songs his characteristic sense of humor, irony, and tightly-wound critical nature. When asked which of his own songs David had most favored, Lisa responded: "He felt about his music like he felt about himself--never satisfied, never good enough." Even his raucous roof-raising songs like *Holes in Yer Head* never let the listener forget that life can leave you black and blue:

Like the big guy said
Be glad you ain't dead
Gotta let the pain out
Through the holes in yer head.

"They mostly reveal his hopelessness about people, himself, and life in general. But they also reveal his connection with and belief in the Spirit world among us," Lisa observes. Among the songs in which the composer is painfully seeking the peace the world does not give is *Clear Blue Sky*. Written before 9/11, it speaks of bombs dropping from an innocent sky and people pining for:

Something wise, maybe something sacred
I don't know. How would I know?
Something to wash away hatred.
I don't know. How would I know?

In his song *Once in Awhile*, David seeks redemption but cannot quite let go of his skepticism which remains rooted in his sense of unworthiness:

I've got a reason to be skeptical.
I've got a reason to believe
That once in awhile
I need a divine intervention.
Don't need no mountain to climb.
How 'bout a dose of redemption?

Lisa points out that the only song David ever admitted having written for someone in particular was his understated love song *Concrete Roses*. His former wife says that he changed the lyrics before recording the song on a "Checkers" CD. "He didn't want anyone to know his deepest feelings for me. I remember the original by heart. He may have those lyrics written down somewhere--unless he destroyed all the evidence as he did with his cell phone because the correspondence on that would have shown who he truly was, how he truly felt."

Here Lisa quotes the first verse of *Concrete Roses* in its original form. The title refers to a cement garden statue David gave Lisa of a boy offering a girl a bouquet of roses.

Heaven sent, heaven knows
Love like rays through windows
Tore down my shades
Tore down my walls
I give you a dozen concrete roses.

By contrast, the lyrics David sang and published were much less revealing of the deep commitment he felt but dared not publicly speak:

A beauty seen, a beauty known
Neither fades, neither's worn
A beauty shared but ours alone
I give you a dozen concrete roses.

Lisa emphasizes that just as David's lyrics often reveal his inner life, his guitars were an extension of himself. "They were as necessary for his health and well-being as oxygen. They were his security in this world. Creating and performing with his guitars was his only healthy outlet for experiencing joy."

Sharing David's career as a musician, giving him feedback on his performances, dancing to his music at wedding receptions and concerts and clubs, his extroverted and life-loving wife often reveled in the good times his bands created for others.

Despite the recurrent difficulties and two wrenching divorces, Lisa does not remember David with regret. "The parts and places inside me that I love the most were reached through my loving and trying relationship with your beloved son," she wrote to me. "For that, I am thankful and eternally grateful."

Three voices--a boyhood admirer, a fellow musician, a former wife--witness how their lives would have been poorer had they not known David. As George Bailey's angel avers, "Each man's life touches so many other lives. When he isn't around, he leaves an awful hole."

If only David had known it.

If only he had believed it.

CHAPTER 7

SOUL IMAGES

Because true belonging only happens when
we present our authentic, imperfect selves to
the world, our sense of belonging can never
be greater than our level of self-acceptance.

Bréne Brown

One of the inherent dangers in writing a memoir of a suicide is that we are so consumed by sorrow and confusion about why it happened that death monopolizes the story. David's family and friends know that he was so much more than a gunshot in a dark woods. He had a full life before he ended it at the age of 48.

I recall having heard that Native Americans of the past two centuries often denied photographers the privilege of taking their pictures. They believed that the camera was stealing their souls. In time, the majority came to see their own portraits as visible links to their honored ancestors. The camera was no longer a thief but a chronicler.

Our family albums, the "hard copies" with plastic wrapped pages and gold embossed covers, are our chronicle of David. Might they not reflect or at least suggest the state of his soul at various stages in his life? I decided to take the risk of searching through those pages in the hope that I would find more comfort than anguish.

The quotations to which I have pegged each picture are reflections of the deeper truths hindsight suggests about what the camera saw.

Music expresses that which cannot be put into words and that which cannot remain unsaid.

--Victor Hugo

1. Here is Davy on the verge of three years old, the youngest child at the Christ Child Day Nursery in Plattsburgh, NY. He has been chosen to lead the Christmas parade and he takes his responsibilities with great seriousness. The Little Drummer Boy's intensity in performing for an audience hints at the way in which music will become his primary language of connecting with others. His innate shyness cowers before the bravado of the drum. He is determined to do it right.

How we need another soul to cling to.

-Sylvia Plath

2. Davy is about ten. He's preparing to wash the El Camino. His wan look of resignation is painful to see. Was he wishing he had a brother or sister to share the chore? I think it is much deeper than that. It was a loneliness that was as much a part of him as his blue eyes and blond hair. It was an existential awareness that each of us, whether in a large family or a monk's hermitage, is alone in this world. The photo seems eerily prophetic now. I see him walking into the night woods with a gun in his pocket and a world weary expression on his face.

*"Giving your son a skill is better
than giving him a thousand pieces
of gold."*

(Chinese proverb)

3. A few years later here is David in white overalls swinging an axe with a block of wood stuck on its head. His father is pretending to beat him to the punch with his chain saw. David is enjoying the joke while doing his part in fitting up the winter's supply of wood. In a companion picture (not shown here), he is scraping plaster to expose the fireplace in our 1810 house in Brunswick. He wanted to be useful, and needed to be affirmed in his efforts to learn several of the trades in which his father was skilled.

Loneliness is not cured by human company. [It] is cured by contact with reality.

--Anthony de Mello

4. His senior portrait taken at Cheverus High, a Jesuit school in Portland, ME, is somber. His expression is studiously blank like that of an actor making sure that he does not telegraph his true intent. Perhaps the photographer said "Smile" and David had his own idea about how he wanted to appear. He has grown a light moustache, unmistakable mark of manhood. Here is the one who, in the eyes of those who love him, is becoming the "beautiful and brilliant" person who will be eulogized 30 years later.

*Man cannot long separate himself
from nature without withering as a
cut rose in a vase.*

--Howard Thurman

5. The photo of David at 20 reveals a young man whose life has gotten off track after he began drinking heavily and dropped out of college. His hair is raggedy; his clothes unkempt. He is in Fort Kent, ME where he is helping his father build a house overlooking the St. John River. A chickadee had flown into the unfinished structure and lost his bearings. David gently caught him and cupped him in his long-fingered hands. He looks down fondly at the befuddled black-capped creature. Throughout his life, David saved birds, small animals and insects. He declined to take up the tradition of deer hunting which his father's family valued.

There is nothing small in the service of God.

--St. Francis de Sales

6. Several years later, here is David at his first wedding reception. He and Deena Dubois have just been married at St. Louis Church in Fort Kent, ME. Looking princely in his silver grey tuxedo, he is dancing with our long-time friend, Helen Small. His face is totally attentive, undistracted by a hall filled with younger guests. As Barbara Yuodsnukis would later say in her eulogy, "David was an intent listener and a thoughtful responder. He had the gift of being friendly and inviting to people of all ages." What Barbara did not know was that one of young David's first folk guitar gigs was at a nursing home in York, ME. There he played his acoustic Yamaha to accompany the old folks' hymn singing. After the prayer service, he went from room to room with our friend Naomi Burton Stone (herself in her 70s), playing for those who could not leave their beds.

*I can't tell my children to
reach for the sun.
All I can do is reach for it myself.*

--Joyce Maynard

7. September 1989. David has just put down the baby car seat in
which his and Deena's newborn daughter is sitting, staring up at
him with bright eyes and a pacifier in her mouth. David is all in
black and wearing his John Lennon glasses. He is looking at the
camera but clearly not seeing anything. He has retreated into his
thoughts. Thank God, he does not know that he will be separated from Kirsten for much of her childhood. Nor can he then
imagine that she will one day follow him in choosing music as her
life's work/joy.

Certain it is that there is no kind of affection so purely angelic as of a father to a daughter . . .there is something which there are no words to express.

--Joseph Addison

8. It is May 1992 and Kirsten has come to see her father for her Easter visit. She is wearing a flouncy pink and blue girly-girly dress and her head is a mass of blonde curls bouncing freely about. David is leaning over his daughter, miming her soap opera headache pose with his right hand held dramatically to the forehead. They love playing off each other and will continue to do so into her adulthood. David's face is lit with deep affection.

*Children are the hands by which we
take hold of heaven.*

Henry Ward Beecher

9. Five years later David is sitting on our backyard swing with Kirsten on one side, his second daughter Jessica on the other, and Grandma Gloria ("Mimi") on the left. Jessy's mother is David's long-term friend Sheri Danner. They will remain friends for several years but then drift apart. David has a wooden cross hanging around his neck. He has been playing with Kirsten and Jessy, making them laugh. He never needs to drink when he is with his daughters. For now, he is blessedly in touch.

*The secret of a happy marriage
remains a secret.*

Henny Youngman

10. Here he is at his second wedding with his new bride Lisa Gagnon. She and David and Kirsten are wound up in delight. In his black tux, David looks like a man who knows his place in the world. Lisa's extroverted, life-loving nature draws him out of himself. Loneliness is held at bay for a time. Several years later David and Lisa will divorce, remain friends, and then re-marry for a short time.

"Drunkenness is temporary suicide: the happiness that it brings is merely negative, a momentary cessation of unhappiness."

(Bertrand Russell)

11. David, Bill (Gehring) and Bruce (Nadeau) are celebrating fellow musician Mike E. C.'s birthday at a California club. They have performed together for years as Bruce and the Crewcuts, and then as The Checkers. At this time, he often drinks too much at the bars where his bands play. However, he says he can and does go without drinking "whenever he decides to" do so. No worries.

"Artistic temperament sometimes seems a battleground, a dark angel of destruction and a bright angel of creativity."

--Madeleine L'Engle

12. David is in his Furball Studio wearing a headset and watching the console with the same intensity he projected as the Little Drummer Boy. He is now deeply involved in learning and applying principles of sound engineering. His friend Jim will later tell us that David drank habitually when he wasn't working on his music. "He was never satisfied with a track, never thought it was quite good enough," Jim adds.

There was comfort in rummaging through the albums, finding photos of our son at his ease with us and others. There was anguish in seeing his solitary nature, his pulling away from the connections he needed, and his striving for perfection as a man and as a musician/composer/sound engineer.

Months after David's death, I came across an observation that Marilynne Robinson, a favorite writer of mine, had made in an interview with *Paris Review*. She said that if we think "only faultless people are worthwhile" we are committing "an incredible exclusion of almost everything of deep value in the human saga."

Did David work so hard at getting everything right because he thought love and a secure sense of belonging had to be earned? Was he convinced that he somehow did not deserve to be loved as so many of us loved him?

The camera was indeed a helpful chronicler of David's life. But it did not steal his soul. That remains as great a secret as it was throughout his 48 years.

Keeping himself to himself was his primary addiction.

CHAPTER 8

SEEKING OBLIVION

*It's so much darker when a light goes
out than it would have been if it had
never shone.*

--John Steinbeck

When I came across an unusual method of recognizing personality types several years ago, I immediately told David about the enneagram. He was often attracted by sources of knowledge which were meaningful but as yet undiscovered by most people. The enneagram (from the Greek for "nine" and "figure") is a tool for the "reading of souls" based on ancient wisdom sources. Its purpose is to provide guidance in self-discovery and spiritual development leading to transformation. It was right up David's alley.

After studying the nine possible enneagram types on the circle chart, our son had no trouble identifying himself as a Type #5, often called "The Observer" or "The Investigator." Fives are motivated by a desire to be capable of meeting whatever demands life makes of them. They need to understand how the world works so that they can feel more secure and useful in society.

The way they go about amassing knowledge often paradoxically isolates them from family and friends, the very ones they most need to connect with. When David decided to teach himself how to be a competent sound engineer, he became a comparative hermit. When he was working on an original rock CD, his band mates rarely saw him between practices. When he agreed to handle the technical production of my self-published book, he periodically ignored my calls and e-mails. Faced with another specialized field to master, he wanted no intrusions.

Type 5s do not swim with the main stream. Whenever our son had made up his mind about something, he could not be budged. Because he lived so much in his head, he was often out of touch with his own and others' feelings. He, like most Type 5s, was never totally free of the conviction that he "didn't belong."

I remember our son's pleasure at learning that among the "Famous 5s" of the enneagram were one of his favorite musicians (John Lennon), most admired film directors (Tim Burton), and Nirvana's lead singer (Kurt Cobain) whose voice he could readily duplicate. What neither of us knew at the time was that the 5s included Vincent van Gogh with whom the presider at David's memorial service would draw a connection.

Not coincidentally, Cobain and van Gogh took their own lives. Recently I reviewed the levels of integration and disintegration at which 5s may find themselves. In David's early adulthood, I could see several of the positive qualities of his personality type. He was open-minded, curious, quirkily humorous, enigmatic and capable of producing impressive original music, posters and cartoons. His ideas about music, art, pop culture, philosophy and religion were often ahead of the times. He was an engaging conversationalist when he felt like connecting.

On the opposite end of the scale, in mid-life, when alcohol began to take him down further than he had been before, he could be antagonistic, cynical, impatient with the thick-headed, provocative toward the politically unenlightened, suspicious of others' motives, and ready to reject a friend or lover who did not measure up.

He who had always been nonviolent, calm in emergencies, courageous when confronted, became fearful of an armed robbery at the family convenience store where he worked or at his upstairs apartment. He clearly felt threatened. So he bought a gun from a customer. We never thought of it as having any other purpose than self-defense.

At the lowest level of disintegration for 5s, *The Wisdom of the Enneagram* (Don Richard Riso and Russ Hudson, Bantam 1999) lists the following dire characteristics: "Seek oblivion; Explosively self-destructive; May commit suicide."

After David's self-inflicted death, my sister Carole gave me Judy Collins' book *Sanity & Grace: A Journey of Suicide, Survival, and Strength.* Collins narrates the story of her son Clark's suicide and her own addictions. She speculates that Clark might never have been able to set his own boundaries. And she is reminded of a Bruce Coburn lyric: "I never knew what you wanted, so I gave you everything" (p. 44).

In hindsight, I realize that our son had rarely denied us anything of importance that we asked of him. When Dave decided to sell the family business, it was David who said, "Let me take it over, Dad." He thought that his father would really prefer to keep the store in the family. His wife Lisa later told us that "he wanted to make his father proud of him."

David stuck with it for five years until he was visibly burned out and drinking heavily. It was during this same period that he offered to design and produce my book of spiritual reflections. In his own way, he gave us everything he had to give.

In *Sanity & Grace*, Judy Collins refers to the "unconscious suicidal urge" that plagued her and her son. She notes that Carl Jung described that urge as "a fatal resistance to life in this world" (p. 21.)

My heart bounded when I read that phrase. It was a perfect reference to an Enneagram 5 who has reached disintegration. And it translated for me the words that came out of my mouth when David's body was found.

"He could no longer live this life."

CHAPTER 9

SEEKING PEACE

*No person is in such darkness as
to be completely devoid of divine
light. The divine light shines in the
darkness and radiates upon all.*

St. Thomas Aquinas

Until our son killed himself, no one ever confided in us that they had a family member or friend who had done the same. No one had ever entrusted to us the story of his or her own attempts at self-annihilation. The term "suicide" is so laden with shame that few people will use it in reference to themselves or to a lost loved one.

They may bemoan the self-inflicted loss of a Kurt Cobain or a Matthew Warren. But they rarely tell the truth about how a husband or wife intentionally took an overdose of sleeping pills or drove the family car off a cliff. Suicide has been called "the last taboo in American society."

What follows is a sampling of the stories people have told us since David's death. A few of them are confessions, stories that have not been told before but kept hidden away like bodies buried in the backyard. The final story, "The Anorexic," has been openly shared to honor the lost son.

Our hope is that the telling of these wounding experiences may encourage readers to share any of their own untold stories of attempted suicides or of loved ones who have succeeded in taking their own lives.

1 The Bridge

Shortly after David's memorial service, our friends Bruce and Lana Buckley came over for coffee. They had been talking for about two hours when Lana stood up, saying that they had some errands to do. Bruce hung back. His look was sorrowful. I thought he was burdened with memories of David at the convenience store where he had seen him almost daily for five years.

"My older brother Donnie killed himself," he said.

"Oh, Bruce. I'm so sorry."

I instantly understood why it was so hard for others to know what to say to us about David's death. What can anyone say that is an adequate response to an act that is felt by the survivors as an accusation and a betrayal?

"Yeah. It was December five years ago. He jumped off a bridge but as he started his fall, he changed his mind at the last second and grabbed hold of a beam. The police came but they didn't get him down. His fingers got too cold for him to hang on any longer. So he fell."

Although Bruce had not been present at the bridge, he was re-living it as though he had been a witness. His face was contorted by the memory of those who failed to rescue his brother.

In the spring of that year, Bruce had been drinking heavily. He felt a strong urge to go fishing off a bridge he had never before been on. While he was there, a sadness overcame him and he went home to sober off.

The next day he related the story to a friend who asked, "Why in the world did you go fishing there? Didn't you know that's where they found

54

your brother's body last spring?" It had been carried down there by the swollen river.

Bruce's eyes were brimming but his facial muscles had relaxed a bit. "I never talk about it," he said.

2. The Razor Blades

One of the most evident things about Margaret was how devoted she was to her eldest daughter Ruth. They talked daily on the phone whenever Margaret and her husband George were away from home. Whenever her daughter had a problem with her children or her co-workers, Margaret was right there to counsel and comfort her favorite daughter. There was nothing she would not do for her daughter.

When Margaret heard about David's suicide, she invited me to go the movies "to forget our troubles for a few hours." As it turned out, seeing Daniel Day-Lewis in *Lincoln* was less a distraction than a reminder of how a son's death can unhinge a loving parent. I cried over Mary Todd and Abe's loss of their beloved Robert. And I cried bitterly over David's not telling me of his despair and how he planned to end it.

"Gloria," Margaret said, "I've never told anyone this. The only one who knows is George. But now I want you to know because it will help you to understand something."

"What is it?"

"Fifteen years ago this May I was going through a terrible depression. George and I had been fighting and I felt completely alone. Every day was worse than the one before. Finally, I couldn't stand it any more. I locked myself in the bathroom and began slashing my wrists. If George hadn't broken the door open to rescue me, I'd be dead."

"Oh, my God!"

Once again I had no words adequate to respond to my friend.

"The reason I'm telling you is that at the time, I never even thought of Ruth or my other kids. Not once. It was as though they no longer existed. All I knew was my pain and I had to escape from it."

I stared at her, trying to take in the reality of her shutting out her favorite daughter with whom she shared "everything."

"She never knew," Margaret said. "I'm only telling you because you need to understand that it was the same for David. He wasn't thinking about you or Dave or Kirsten or anyone. He was thinking about snuffing out the pain."

I later read the account of a retired professor whose son had hung himself 15 years earlier. The father felt certain that "suicides are so desperate that they don't feel emotional connections to the rest of us and must seek a place where they will belong" (*No Time to Say Good-bye*, Carla Fine, p. 141).

That rang true for our son as well. I will never forget Margaret's courageous admission to me, a truth which to this day the person closest to her in the world knows nothing about.

The Sleeping Pills

We had not seen our friends for many years. They had been divorced for a long time and moved out of state. When the opportunity came to stop by Marilyn's house on our travels, I took it in the hope of renewing an old friendship. She was delighted to brew us some Starbucks and break open a bag of Pepperidge Farm cookies.

For the first hour, Marilyn kept the conversation riding smoothly over the familiar roads of family and our respective part-time retirement jobs. Then, after a nervous pause, she asked, "So, how are you doing?"

I had heard that question, word for word, so many times that I thought it must appear in a book of etiquette on "How to Talk to a Bereaved Parent of a Suicide." I never knew what to say. If I answered it honestly, the questioner would visibly draw back, trying to think of some way to cut me off at the pass. So I usually settled for, "As well as can be expected."

To which they replied with some variation of "Well, don't worry. Time heals all wounds. You'll feel better soon."

But Marilyn had no intention of subverting the truth. She invited me to express my grief and did not turn away from my weeping. Once again I was most hurt by David's not confiding in me, not giving me any indication of what he planned to do, not seeking my help or intercession in any way. My son whom I considered my closest friend shut me out of the most momentous event of his entire life!

Marilyn took my hand. Her voice was calm and considered.

"There is something I have to tell you. I've never told anyone else. I was too ashamed."

"What is it?" Even as I asked, I knew what was coming. Not the details. Just the act itself.

"When Sam and I were going through the divorce, I moved into an apartment and the kids stayed with me. Even though I was the one who initiated the divorce, I tried to reconcile with him. But he wouldn't budge."

Marilyn's face flushed as she revealed a truth she chronically kept hidden even from herself.

"I felt like I was dying. I still loved Sam and I didn't know how I was going to live without him. I got so depressed I had to have a neighbor take the kids for a few days. I couldn't go to work yet I couldn't lose my job either. I didn't know what to do. I was absolutely desperate. So I emptied out a bottle of sleeping pills and began taking them one by one until I passed out. My neighbor found me and called the ambulance."

I put my arms around her but she held back.

"But here's the part I want you to know. Even though I loved my kids and would have done anything for them, I did not give them a single thought. Not them. Not my parents or my sister. My mind was completely taken over by despair. I had no hope. No future. All I wanted was peace. I had to have peace. I'm so ashamed!"

We wept together over her younger self and my son and all the other sufferers who daily face the demons of hopelessness.

"Thank you for telling me, Marilyn," I said, "I am so grateful for your honesty."

"I just hope it helps you," she replied, knowing that she was practicing a kind of pay-it-forward in the company of suicides and their survivors.

4 The Stolen Gun

It happened 29 years ago. There are days, even weeks, when the thought of her does not invade their present space. But when the opportunity to tell Sheila's story arises, the memory of how she left them still hurts. They are willing to bear it for the sake of their daughter and for those who may be helped by hearing her story.

Ed and Kathy Dyson lost their first child at seven months. "When I was four months pregnant with Sheila, I found my son, Billy, dead in his crib. He had been born with severe birth defects. While Billy never grew beyond 10 pounds and only smiled for the first time the night before he died, he was beautiful to look at, blond and always a newborn. I often wondered if this period of severe grief affected Sheila in her fetal development," Kathy says.

When Sheila was born in 1965, she was the picture of health and vigor. She walked at nine months and began talking soon thereafter. Her mother describes her as "strong-willed from birth," comparing her to the little girl in the old rhyme who "when she was good, she was very, very good, and when she was bad, she was horrid." Sheila's conviction that she knew her own mind remained her primary characteristic throughout her short life.

Sheila's brother Thom was born 11 1/2 months after her. He looked so much like a healthy version of Billy that friends of the family would often call him by his departed brother's name. Thom and Sheila became close friends, and it was to him that she gave her few material treasures when she decided to end her life.

After the Dysons moved to Maine in 1978, Sheila joined a church folk group and learned to play guitar. "Her voice was beautiful,"

Kathy recalls. "She would go on to write songs and some were very good because they were based on her personal experience. Even with an IQ of 140, she somehow didn't seem to be able to handle life on an even keel."

Kathy is referring to her daughter's mood swings and recurring need for a psychological counselor which began when she was nine. "Months of counseling followed by apparent improvement led to her being released which was then followed by months of decline that eventually led to more counseling. Somewhere along the way, she attempted suicide for the first time."

At the age of 15, Sheila became pregnant with a son, "David." Her parents decided to place her in a Catholic home for unwed mothers where they knew she would receive compassionate care and mental health assistance that might "finally break through to her needs," her mother says. David was born on August 12, 1980, the exact date of the month on which his young mother would complete suicide four years later.

At 17 Sheila gave birth to Veronica. The father of the child showed no interest in her, so Ed and Kathy welcomed their daughter and granddaughter into their home. "It was a very happy time for all of us--for just about a year. Then Sheila went into decline again. That led to Veronica's being adopted by the same family who had adopted David." Losing her granddaughter at 18 months again plunged Kathy Dyson into mourning. "It was all the same emotions and pain as the death of my son."

Sheila began another downward spiral. She was 19 and her parents could not prevent her from leaving home. Later she called from Texas to say that she was broke and stuck in a motel.

"My brother Matt lives in Texas so he and his wife drove for hours to pick Sheila up. It was Matt who called to tell us that she had killed herself. The police were there when he and his wife arrived at the motel. Sheila had hitchhiked. The trucker who gave her a ride showed off a .357 Magnum he carried. When the opportunity presented itself, she stole it. We know because we were still standing by the phone after the call about her suicide and it was the driver looking for her and his gun. She had given him our phone number. It was her son David's birthday."

Ed and Kathy went from disbelief to numbness to "relief of a sort" that their daughter was now beyond her suffering. "It took a long time to get over the guilt this feeling gave me, and to accept it as O.K. Then the hollowness of grief set in. I had never seen Ed in such pain," she says.

The three family members who survived Sheila Dyson were "held aloft" by their church community and, for Thom, the college community which he had just entered as a freshman. "Our church was unbelievably supportive," Kathy recalls. "It still takes my breath away and brings tears to my eyes. The foundations were laid for long, close friendships. Such treasures on earth!"

In the note Sheila left, she asked "I was a good mother, wasn't I?" Kathy replies in capital letters: "YES! By allowing her children to be born, then letting David go. She was an unbelievably good mom to Veronica that first year, far surpassing our expectations. Then by doing what she knew was the best thing for her child, letting Veronica have a chance at a good home and upbringing, was the most loving act a mother could do."

It took several years for Kathy Dyson to accept the reality that she "did the best I could with who I was at the time, but I was not enough to provide for all of Sheila's needs. And it was not my fault that she killed herself."

Twenty-nine years after their only daughter shot herself in a Texas motel room, Kathy and Ed Dyson are inclined to remember Sheila primarily at times of family celebrations. Her mother says, "She loved parties. It is the good times I mostly remember, and they were plentiful."

The bereaved mother pauses. Then she concludes, "But I still miss what she might have become."

5 The Anorexic

Shortly after our David's death, a friend in Virginia put me in touch with Jeanne and Joe Mitcho whose 34-year old only son Seth had died on

October 6, 2010. He had struggled with anorexia for eight years. When I wondered whether there was a parallel between David's and Seth's deaths, Joe responded:

"There's some difference between our sons' passing, but not as much as you think. When a son is a friend and companion and can't do what he needs to do to reach out for help--well, it's not a lot different. . .Two years later, we're still crying. . .You can only guess what courage it took for your son David to make it to the day it finally became too much."

Joe was the first person to mention "courage" in connection with David's death. He and Jeanne knew what bravery had been required of their son as death approached. When the Mitchos told me more of Seth's story, I immediately saw how our sons mirrored each other in their brain-iness, determined need for control over their own lives, and fatal conviction that they knew what was best for them.

Although Seth, unlike David, had received the best of professional care, including two hospitalizations at Johns Hopkins Eating Disorder Unit, his mother says "I think he believed he 'out analyzed' them all." Jeanne then adds, "He never denied his sickness; he only denied that he would die from it." (Anorexia causes a greater number of deaths than any other form of mental illness. And, as Joe points out, "it can eat up those around it's main target." They constantly begged Seth to eat--to no avail.)

The Mitchos were repeatedly heartbroken when they saw their son, a successful young business analyst, losing weight and trying to deal with his illness. "He would get scared, take a leave of absence from work, begin seeing a therapist, nutritionist, but he would soon begin 'manipulating 'them, and before long, he was back where he started," Jeanne recalls.

Because the family had a firm habit of "full disclosure," they talked openly with Seth about his illness and their fears about what it was doing to him. His mother had nightmares about finding him unresponsive at the bottom of his townhouse stairs. On the weekend before he died, Seth sent Jeanne an e-mail with an uncharacteristically brief message:

"Mom, I know you think I love ED [a term the parents used for eating disorder] more than you, but that's just not true!"

Neither of the Mitchos were prepared when a policeman knocked at their door at 6:30 a.m. on October 6 and informed them of their son's death. His girlfriend had found him lifeless in front of his TV. "I was in total denial until that moment," Joe says. "ED was stronger than we were and much more persuasive."

Jeanne had enjoyed a rare deep sleep the night of October 5. "I believe that my uncharacteristic calm before Seth died was, in some way, a message that his pain by then was so intense that I needed to step back and unselfishly let him go back to God. I think that after years of starvation, he was just tired of the fight. I think his heart just stopped."

At Seth's funeral liturgy, his younger sister Sara gave a eulogy in which she confessed her anger at her brother for allowing himself to slip away. "I fought with him for his life," she said, acknowledging that "the other side of anger is love." Noting how much Seth loved puzzles, she commented "He was a puzzle himself. . .and he's given us all different answers to his puzzle and all of the answers we've found are the right ones."

The celebrant, Fr. Charley Miller, recognized how many times during the previous eight years Seth's family and close friends must have told themselves, "Certainly my love should be able to touch him, to save him." He recognized their frustration, sadness and anger at Seth's inexorable journey away from them. But Seth, like each of us, was a mystery.

"We can guess, you had a glimpse, of the pain Seth endured, but no one can ever know the depths he faced in the lonely moment of the night. We can guess, you had a glimpse, of the courage he showed, but no one can ever fully know the shining courage that Seth summoned up to face another day, to connect with you as much as he could, to keep on keeping on, to believe, to hope. Only he knows that, and his God. For the mystery of the human person, like Seth, is the image of the mystery of God."

With the beacon of hindsight, Joe and Jeanne Mitcho shared a few insights into the grieving process and what they have learned from it so far.

Jeanne compares grief to "a treasured photo kept in a box." She is careful about when and how often she opens that box. She is careful "about when [she allows] the eyes, the smile, the touch, the voice of the person in that photo. . .to reach into [her] soul and transport [her]to a place of loss [she'd] rather not go."

Joe's grieving "doesn't end and I don't want it to," he says. He needs family and friends who are willing to talk candidly and without discomfort about Seth, his life, and how he died. He advises other parents in the same situation to "feel what you feel," hold on to the memories (good and not-so-good), and treasure your "sense of what may be after this life."

Seth's father wonders if the two of them "will be reconnected as individuals [in the after life] or as a total consciousness of which we're both a part." He wonders if he really believes in the communion of saints (all those who went before us and are yet to come), and if he "should be mad at God, whoever HE/SHE is." And he reminds himself to get ready for his own death by living each day as fully as he can.

Jeanne Mitcho advises parents to accept the reality that they have done their best with their lost son or daughter, and to recognize that "sometimes we just stand powerless before the mystery." Asked how her own faith has been affected by Seth's death, she responds:

"I question prayer in ways that I never did. My family, friends and I prayed as no one ever could for Seth's recovery. He prayed as well. When I hear people say, 'God heard our prayers and my daughter's tumor was not cancer,' I want to say, 'God didn't hear my prayers. . .and my son died.' Are we praying to the same God? And is that God playing favorites, or not always paying attention? That's not a theology I can embrace."

Despite her pain, Jeanne continues to believe in the God who is Love. Rather than praying as she did before, she practices being present to the Mystery. She believes firmly in our connection with those who have died, a connection she continues to experience with her son "not on demand" but when she least expects it.

The Mitchos are grateful for their faith community at St. Francis of Assisi Church in Triangle, VA. Their fellow parishoners accept the Mitchos' doubts and willingly struggle with the big questions while celebrating the graced moments of God's presence among them.

His parents view Seth Mitcho's final refusal to seek any more professional help for his mental illness not so much as choosing death as "choosing peace" or "being chosen by death."

Although I have never met Joe and Jeanne Mitcho, I know that if I ever do, we will embrace each other as old friends who have survived the same battle and lived to tell about it. I am also certain that our cherished sons now know each other as brothers in the communion of saints which will one day gather us all in.

Until then, we tell our stories and shelter each other against the unrelenting chill of grief.

CHAPTER 10

COUNTING THE WAYS

How do I love thee? Let me count the ways.

Elizabeth Barrett Browning

Few of us emerge from our high school English classes without reading, reciting or analyzing Elizabeth Barrett Browning's Sonnet 43: *How do I love thee?* It is a romantic classic enumerating the ways in which the poet is devoted to the love of her life, Robert Browning. Because her poem is spiritual as well as romantic, it speaks powerfully of true love's immortality. She promises her husband-to-be that she will love him even "better after death."

I wish there were a poem of equal stature that expressed a parent's devotion to a child, especially a child who takes his or her own life. But I could neither find one nor write one. However, both Dave and I could "count the ways" in which we had always and would always love our only son.

We could do it through selected anecdotes that shine in the dark halls of memory like vigil lights at midnight. Slight as they are, these stories carry the weight of our combined affection for David. And they help us to recognize his enduring presence in our lives.

We love you for the child in you that did not fade away.

Often when you were with your daughters you were their age only taller. On the frozen pond behind our house in Carthage, ME, you became an Olympic figure skater whose wobbly arabesques and pigeon-toed racing made little Kirsten and Jessy feel confident that they could do at least that well--as soon as they stopped laughing. In Kirsten's teen years, her visits with you were highlighted by the karate routines the two of you devised. Your mutual side thrust kicks and spear hand thrusts were wildly exaggerated, and accompanied by macho yells of "High-Ya!" Kirsten sometimes fell on the floor gasping with laughter at your contortions.

We love you for the originality of your thinking which did not fade away.

When you were five, I noticed that you had constructed an impressive tower with your legos. The following dialogue ensued.

Mom: "You're quite a builder."

Davy: "Yes, I was for years."

Mom: "You were?"

Davy: "Yes, when I was a baby I was. But I didn't build because I knew I was a baby."

Mom: "Oh, I see."

Davy: "Maybe God taught me."

Mom: "I wouldn't be surprised."

Davy: "Maybe that's the way he does with children."

Mom: "That sounds right."

We love you for your dry wit that did not fade away.

Once, when you were about six, you deliberately ignored some directive from Daddy. When he repeated his request and it remained undone, he said, "Do you want a spanking?" You looked at him, thought it over for a second, and replied, "No thanks. Maybe later."

A few years earlier when we were invited to dinner at your godmother's house, Daddy said to you on departure, "Aren't you going to thank

Betsy for the dinner?" Without missing a beat, you piped up, "Thanks for the dinner, Betsy. It wasn't very good but I ate it anyway."

We blushed at your audacity but had to admit to ourselves that your critique was on target. Betsy's culinary skills were limited at the time, and her spaghetti sauce would have held up in court as proof that she was practicing without a license.

We love you for your inner calm in all emergencies which did not fade away.

When you were in fourth or fifth grade, I parked our Mach-1 Mustang in the driveway and we both got out. As I headed for the front door, you said matter-of-factly, "Mom, I think the car is on fire."

"What?"

"The car's on fire. You go call the fire station. I'll get the neighbor."

Scared into submission by the billowing smoke and your adult demeanor, I did as I was told. The neighbor was afraid "to get involved," but the fire department was prompt and no one suffered anything other than frayed nerves and diminished respect (for the neighbor).

Another time during that same stage of your life, we were coming home from Plattsburgh after spending Christmas with your grandparents. Dad was driving the Ford Escort and we had just crossed into Maine from New Brunswick. Suddenly, as we started down a steep incline, we realized that the entire road was a sheet of black ice.

"Well, we're in trouble now," Dad said in a tone that told us fervent prayer was in order.

To gain any control over the veering Escort, Dad had to accelerate. We were barreling down the hill, lurching from one side of the road to the other.

My face must have revealed the terror I felt because you took my hand, held it firmly, and said in a confident voice, "It's alright, Mom. We'll be alright."

I clasped your hand until we had reached the bottom of the hill and Dad had pulled off to the side of the road. He laughed with relief, I cried for the same reason, and you shook your hand energetically, pretending that I had cut off all your circulation with my death grip.

Your calm was our anchor.

We love you for your patience in teaching us how to find our way around a computer, an iPhone, or a sound system which did not fade away.

You were always our go-to tech guy from the time we were mystified by our first Bose sound system in an RV to the day, within a month of your dying, when you gave your father an iPhone and explained its mysterious intricacies..

If some of our questions identified us as first graders in Computers 101, you never let on. You understood that we had not grown up in a digital age. Nor were you blind to how the gathering years clouded our ability to catch on quickly to new information.

The best example of how you mentored us with infinite forbearance was the time several years ago when my publisher finally insisted that I switch from an electronic typewriter to a computer. I dreaded letting go of my long-familiar writing process over which I felt I had complete control. The computer was about to take charge. I was scared witless.

For the first week or so, every lesson was aborted by my repeated cries of "I don't get it" and "That doesn't make any sense." The frustration was unbearable. Tears rolled down my face as you quietly explained once again how to forward a chapter to the publisher.

"It's O.K., Mom. That's enough for today" you would say, in that even-tempered voice that assured me my anguish was not dismissed as a childish whim.

Your patience paid off, son. My computer and I are now on intimate terms, and my day would be incomplete without it.

We love you for your compassion which did not fade away.

There are so many examples of your empathizing with those who, whether through their own fault or society's injustices, needed an advocate or a provider: the children of low-income families at the child care center where you worked, the part-time employees at our store who ran out of cash and required a "loan," the unemployed customers who couldn't afford their morning coffee and donut, the single mothers who brought their little ones into the store to delight in your attention and their favorite treats.

But the example that I pray will be preserved in my memory even if Alzheimer's sets in is the vigil you kept with your grandmother on the night of September 14, 1994. My mother, Pearl Capone, was dying of an intestinal cancer. She had been diagnosed three months earlier, been under Hospice care for over a month, and was now hospitalized in a final attempt to give her respite from unbearable pain.

Everyone in the family was exhausted. We had reached the point of praying for her death ("Please make her let go!") while feeling certain that she would continue suffering for weeks to come. It felt like an overdue birth. We needed the oblivion of sleep.

When the third shift Hospice nurse arrived at 11 p.m., you sensed that your parents and your Aunt Carole were too depleted to remain at Nana's bedside any longer. Although you too had been there for hours, you insisted that we go home. "I'm a night owl," you said. "It's no problem for me."

You sat there, bent forward over the railing of her hospital bed, watching her ravaged face as intently as a mother eagle eyes her fledgling as it attempts its first flight. "Fly away, home, Nana," you implored her. "Fly away home."

The Hospice nurse rubbed your back as the hours passed and you retained your inclined sentinel's position on the ramparts between life and death. At 3:22 a.m. Nana opened her eyes. Within seconds, she focused on your face.

"It's you," she said.

She gave you a little girl smile and squeezed your hand.

You held your breath, smiled back, urged her on with your eyes.

And she went home.

The nurse held you by the shoulders as you wept in relief, sorrow, and disbelief that your beloved grandmother would no longer be standing in the kitchen at 15 Champlain Street when you walked through the back door on one of your occasional visits.

Then you called to tell us, "She's gone."

Later when you narrated the story to me, I urged you to write it down before you started to forget the details. "I don't need to write it down," you said. "I will not forget."

And I'm sure you never did, son. Just as I am sure that Nana must have been the first to welcome you into whatever realm your spirit now calls home.

How do we love you?

We have only begun to count the ways.

CHAPTER 11

BREAKING FAITH

'Son, why have you done this to us?'

Luke 2:48 (NAB)

Dear David Lorne,

The experts all agree. Anger is a required course for those who hope to graduate from the School of Grief. And for those of us whose sons and daughters have killed themselves, not suppressing our anger is crucial to our healing.

You don't need to ask, "Why anger?," do you? You know that suicide imposes a legacy of confusion, accusation, guilt, self-doubt and self-recrimination on the loved ones who are left behind, wringing their hands and suppressing an urge to bang their heads on the wall. Your question ought to be, "Why wouldn't they be angry?"

When you went off to college at the age of 19, I wrote you a letter in the style of Victorian parents who sent their offspring out into the world with an epistle of appreciation and counsel. I praised your accomplishments as a student, an athlete, and a musician. I gave you all the reasons why your father and I were so pleased with you as our son. And I admitted how lost we were going to be without you.

Now you have left us so irretrievably that we have to decide, every morning, to live for one more day. With our morning coffee, we have to swallow the bitter reality that we are going to be without you for the duration of our time on earth.

Yes, we know you are here in spirit. But we need you here "with skin on."

So this is a letter from an angry, ticked off, wounded, deprived, confused, resentful and disbelieving mother to her willfully absent son. It has been six months since your death and, until now, I have been angry only at myself.

Now it is your turn. So, you listen, and listen well.

My best friend betrayed me. He left me without so much as a backward glance. He was so determined not to be detected or detained that he went out the bulkhead door of the basement and stuck a wash cloth in the door to avoid its making a single sound.

When I saw the movie *Life of Pi* a few months after your departure, I was bushwhacked by a scene in which Pi realizes that his tiger companion Richard Parker, with whom he has suffered many trials, has left him. Pi says, "I still cannot understand how he could abandon me so unceremoniously without any sort of goodbye, without looking back even once. That pain is like an axe that chops at my heart."

Are you cringing at the raw emotionalism of it, son? Do you presume that Yann Martel (Pi's creator) and I have overstated the case against friends who betray us? Think again. I don't know how many others feel that you betrayed them by taking your own life. But I am excruciatingly aware that I am one of them.

An axe to the heart. That's what it feels like.

Here is the message from a Mother's Day card you gave me years ago. (I am gathering as many old cards as I can find to console myself every year when the second Sunday in May rolls around. What else am I to do?)

"Mom--All through my life/I've known I could turn to you/to help me/ think things through/or figure out/what direction/was right for me. . ./From the guidance you've offered/to the confidence and wisdom/that you've built in me/you've made me stronger than you know. . ./but never too strong to need/a little help from my mom."

Can you imagine how those words make me wretch now?

In the most important decision you made in your 48 years, you not only did not seek my help, you hoodwinked me. You put on an Academy Award performance as a young man content with the prospect of starting a new era of his life. You led me to believe that you were ready to face the immediate challenge created by your addiction to alcohol and a destructive relationship.

You lied to me and you left me childless!

Yes, I know you are a man. But you will always be my child from here to eternity. So get used to it. No other person in this world bore you in her body for nine months or brought you into this world. You are flesh of my flesh. And I have a right to be flaming mad at you for what you have done.

So you were never too strong to need my help?

Yet you were strong enough to take a loaded gun into the woods, aim it directly at your heart, and pull the trigger. Anyone who says that is an act of cowardice speaks from inexperience.

What was it that bullied you into taking yourself away from us in such a violent and fatal act? I can't believe that it was a free choice because it goes against the grain of your innate goodness--especially to your father and me. I can't believe that you would do anything so horrendous to us if you could avoid it.

Yet you chose not to seek help for your addictions. Over the years you had more than once implied or said outright that you were considering whether you wanted to live or not. Twice you agreed to go to a counselor. Both times you quit the process because the counselor seemed unable to understand or help you. Once you got a DWI and had to go to AA meetings for a short time. You complained that there were "no people like" you there.

You remind me of a line from a Swinburne poem (*April*): "For my heart is set/on what hurts me. . ." Didn't you know that what hurt you hurt us? Didn't you believe that we would have gone to hell and back for you if we'd only known? Didn't you trust that our love for you was indestructible?

You knew how precious your life was.

It was you who taught us that "the price of a life hasn't even told yet."

Or did you forget? Was your vision darkened by despair? Was your heart so swaddled in hopelessness that pity had no place there? Jesus, Mary, and Joseph, don't we deserve to know? Or would knowing kill us too?

My anger burns like a dry oak log when I consider how you left no note of apology or explanation or gratitude or blame. In your last will and testament, you left us only an obligation. Your father is your devastated executor. Perhaps you thought you didn't have anything we needed. How blind you were to our desire to be remembered with some small personal item (a shirt, a book, a piece of jewelry you had worn), a mute declaration of filial love.

You left us without saying good-bye. You denied us an opportunity to help you in your solitary despair. You betrayed me by your calm presence. Your tranquil expression gave your mother and father no reason to worry.

You broke faith with us!

I am trying to forgive you. But you are not off the hook. Your dad and I still walk around in a daze wondering how we got hit by a train when we didn't know we were anywhere near the tracks.

Our short-term memories are shot. We have aged more in the past six months than in the previous six years. We never know when fresh grief will grapple us from behind a song, a movie, an old photograph, an old friend, a sun yellow Jeep like the one you last drove.

After your death, loss became a way of life. We have been prey to all kinds of deprivations ranging from lost sleep to lost keys, lost confidence to lost iPhones, lost caring to lost Medicare cards, lost vision to lost glasses, lost motivation to lost well-being, lost love for life to lost lists of errands, lost memory to lost maps. There is more. But you get the idea.

Your self-inflicted death battered our hearts, clobbered us like the pitiless ultimate fighter suicide is. Your father has seen you in a dream, striding through heaven with your long hair shining and your champagne-colored suit fit for a celestial gig. You haven't yet had the decency to appear to your mother in a single dream.

A few years ago, I gave you a copy of my obituary so that neither you nor Dad would have to compose it when the time came. I was thinking of my own death because a neighbor at our Florida RV park had died suddenly of a heart attack and his family members were all "up north." I told you that I could not bear the thought of dying in Florida without saying good-by to you in Maine.

I hugged you and said, "Just in case anything like that does happen some day, I want you to know that you have been the joy of my life."

You hugged me and said, "Oh, Mom. Me too."

I never once thought of the possibility of your dying before me, dying on purpose, dying by your own gifted hands, leaving me to write your obituary. In the harrowing movie *August: Osage County*, an adult daughter on her way to her father's funeral tells her 14-year old daughter to "Die after me, all right?" She adds, "I don't care what else you do, where you go, how you screw up your life. Just survive. Please."

I know exactly where she was coming from.

You owe me.

Don't forget it.

Love,

Mom

P.S. I just discovered that the card I gave you the day before your death had been put away in your desk drawer by someone who thought they were protecting me from the pain of seeing it there. The card's title was *The Bond Between Mother and Son Lasts a Lifetime*. It points out that a mother's love is "understanding of any situation/and forgiving of any mistake." You left it on the top of your desk where there were no other papers or items of any kind. Now I know that you did leave me a message. And my anger fizzles.

CHAPTER 12

IDENTITY CRISIS

Our truest, deepest self is completely free. It is not crippled or compromised by past actions or concerned with identity or status.

Eben Alexander, M.D.

I f our son had known his truest, deepest self, we would never have had to view his dead body at Brookings-Smith funeral home. We would never have seen his lifeless face, a stranger's face that sickened us by its unfamiliarity. We would never have had to contemplate how he had shot himself in the heart rather than the head because, as his father discerned, "He knew his mother would insist on seeing his body and he did not want to put her through that."

In *Proof of Heaven: A Neurosurgeon's Journey Into the Afterlife*. Eben Alexander heard the following messages as he traveled into "the alternate dimension" many call heaven: "You are loved and cherished, dearly, forever. . .You have nothing to fear. . .There is nothing you can do wrong" (p. 41).

David was deprived of those crucial messages in his final months or maybe years. He had forgotten that he, like each of us, is a reflection of the Divine. His reality radar was out of commission. When a friend accepted his invitation to have a beer after work, the friend said, "Two's my limit." David responded, "When I have one, I can't stop." Yet he refused to see himself as an alcoholic.

Suicide has been called "a meditative act, a noninstinctive, unnatural choice" (Primo Levi). Our son washed and folded all his laundry, packed and marked all of his musical equipment and household items, cleaned out his car, left his bed perfectly arranged, sorted his tools, canceled his car insurance, added his daughter's name to his checking account, listed his passwords for her, left his studio apartment looking as though a realtor was expected at any moment, destroyed his cell phone. He knew well what he was about to do.

At some point, he said to me in a matter-of-fact- tone, "I've made a lot of bad decisions in my life." When I asked for examples, he sidestepped into a generality about "some things I should have done differently." In my maternal haste to assure him that we have all done the same, I missed what might have been an opportunity to hear a revelation. Or perhaps his addiction to secrecy would have ended the discussion exactly as it happened. David lived a well-edited life.

He kept his privacy. And his privacy kept him as isolated as the boy in the glass bubble. We knew he had had two or three flare ups of uncharacteristic anger recently, flare ups in which he spoke and acted with extreme agitation. We attributed these outbursts to his frustrations with the store, and we freed him from those responsibilities as soon as we could by leasing the business rather than waiting for a buyer.

But it was not enough

David decided to take his own life. He saw no other options, or he would have taken one of them. We are trying to accept his leaving us with such brutal finality. As Joan Wickersham, author of *The Suicide Index: Putting My Father's Death in Order*, says it so well: "I accepted everything about him, except that he was the author of his own absence" (p. 104).

As our son lost sight of his true identity as a good man, a loving father and son, a talented musician, a "beautiful and brilliant" person, we now have our own identity crises to face.

If we are to stay alive, be here for his daughters, and do what we can to make his story known as both a tribute to him and a caution to others, we cannot succumb to being secondary victims of a suicide.

Dave and I have each blamed ourselves for what we did and what we failed to do for our son. There is truth in some of our self-accusations. But we are not messiahs capable of saving him. We are not seers who could fathom the horror that was heading our way. We are not neglectful parents who cared little for our only offspring. We simply could not see what we subconsciously feared we could not endure.

That truth was verified for me when I came across a story in Luke's gospel in which Jesus warns his disciples that he is about to be betrayed into the hands of his enemies. He urges them to let his words sink in. But their love for him and their anxiety about what he means blinds them. "And they were afraid to ask him about this saying" (Luke 9:45, NRSV).

Saying these things is an act of faith. If we don't believe them, we can't survive. I will choose to believe an observation made by Carla Fine in her book *No Time to Say Goodbye: Surviving the Suicide of a Loved One*: "Every book on suicide that I have read emphasizes that people who are hell-bent on killing themselves will accomplish it, no matter what you do" (214).

David's self-inflicted death forces us to come to grips with what the meaning of our lives will be without him. How will we keep his memory alive by integrating what was best about him into our own identities? How will we stay connected to our granddaughters and his close friends who want to remain linked to him? How will we do our small part to change society's prejudicial view of suicides and their families? The answers will emerge as we work our way out of grief into a sustainable life.

We cannot allow ourselves to inhabit the identity of guilty parties or helpless victims. If we do, our son's memory will be tarnished. We cannot give up on life. If we do, David will have destroyed three lives. It is up to us to choose whether we see the suffering thrust upon us by a shot fired in the woods at night as a curse or an opportunity.

To put it in its simplest terms: What would David want us to do with the hand he has dealt us?

Perhaps what he wants most of all is our acceptance of his final decision. In an e-mail written a few months after David's death, his former wife Lisa wrote: "I truly believe he was fully present with God and that God was ready for him to come home." Admitting that his death seemed senseless to those of us who "don't want to live life on earth without our beloved," Lisa noted that David would not feel that his death was "senseless."

Speaking of those who take their own lives, she wrote, "They have struggled all their lives to have that sense but could not find their way to peace on earth. So, rather than prolonging the inevitable, they make their own way to peace. There is no fault or blame."

Because Lisa was well aware of how we were faulting ourselves for David's choice, she pointed out that "Contributing to his despair does not control his choices any more than contributing to his happiness. We have no control over another adult. None whatsoever. And that, David was a master of. . .not allowing another person to make him happy or sad."

(David often read and discussed Anthony de Mello, S. J.'s book *Awareness: The Perils and Opportunities of Reality*. The author's goal is to wake people up to the illusions we all live by. He points out that "True happiness is uncaused. You cannot make me happy." When we are in touch with reality, the words and actions of others have no power to control us. We are free to be our true selves.)

Lisa's letter went on to say, "The link that seemed to be missing with him was how to be happy, content, at peace with himself." Like others who have taken their own lives, David "did not have a fulfilling relationship with himself."

In mulling over Lisa's message, an insight passed on by Jeanne Mitcho in her story of her son Seth's death, came to mind. She wrote, "I needed to step back and unselfishly let him go back to God."

Her conclusion led me back to the Lebanese poet Kahlil Gibran whose poem *On Children* appeared on so many posters and plaques in the '60s. He told us that our children, although they came through us, were not ours. They belonged to Life. And we could not keep them with us because "their souls dwell in the house of tomorrow."

We long for the day when we will be reunited with our son in the house of tomorrow.

And we will strive not to be "crippled or compromised" by mourning for a past that will not return.

CHAPTER 13

HOPE SECURED

He alone moulds their hearts: he
understands all they do.

Psalm 33:15 (NJB)

D o suicides go to heaven? Does killing yourself disqualify you as a recipient of God's mercy? These questions trouble almost everyone whose lives are touched by the person who kills himself or herself. Even those of us who declare ourselves certain that God embraces those who take their own lives are haunted by the soft hissings of doubt. We need reassurance because we have been raised with a God cast in our own judgmental image.

The church in which I grew up (Roman Catholic) formerly taught that suicide is a mortal sin. Those who killed themselves were refused a Catholic funeral or a burial in the hallowed ground of a Catholic cemetery.

To reassure myself shortly after David's death, I called an 85-year old priest friend. "Father Gerry, some Catholics still believe that God does not welcome suicides into heaven," I said. His immediate and forceful response was. "Aw, they're nuts!"

He was right. The Church now takes a more compassionate approach. The Catechism of the Catholic Church teaches that God alone knows how the suicide is saved. It observes that those who kill themselves may be victims of "grave psychological disturbances, or have grave fear of hardship" (#2283). They, therefore, have a diminished responsibility for their actions.

Fr. Arnaldo Pangrazzi, international coordinator for the Order of St. Camillus, is the author of a 1988 booklet entitled *Bearing the Special Grief of Suicide*. He points out that suicide is still considered "objectively wrong" but that "individual circumstances may make it subjectively guiltless." He adds that the suicide's grasp of reality may be so weak that he or she cannot be blamed for their actions. "Only God knows what is in the heart of each person."

I am reminded of Willa Cather's novel *My Antonia*. The heroine's father, Mr. Shimerda, finds it impossible to adapt himself to the hardscrabble life of a pioneer in the American West at the turn of the century. At home in Bohemia, he was a successful tailor and violinist. Now he cannot support his family and is deeply depressed.

To the horror of his family, Mr. Shimerda kills himself. As a Catholic, he cannot have a church funeral or be buried in the parish cemetery. At his burial at a local crossroads, Mr. Shimerda is prayed for by the narrator's grandfather.

"Oh, great and just God, no man among us knows what the sleeper knows, nor is it for us to judge what lies between him and Thee."

That prayer assures me that even back in 1918, wise writers like Cather knew that church people needed to outgrow their conviction that suicides were outside God's mercy. To the contrary, I am positive that God sings a special welcome song for those poor souls who arrive with self-inflicted bullet holes and other marks of self-loathing, fear, depression, and despair. (Recall that Jesus himself retained his wounds in his resurrected body.)

How could a loving God who counts all the hairs on our heads (Mt 10:30), who will wipe every tear from our eyes (Ps 25:8a and Rev 7:17b), who tends and heals all our wounds (Jer 30:17 and Ps 147:3) refuse to welcome the brokenhearted son or daughter who could no longer bear his or her life? Ask yourself: Can God be any less merciful than my own mother?

When anyone raises questions about the fate of suicides, I remind them that Jesus himself said that he came not for the people who are healthy and have it all together. They have no need of a doctor. But the sick do. (See Mk 2:17.) I refer them to a verse in Timothy assuring us that God remains faithful to us, no matter what, "for he cannot disown his own self" (2 Tm 2:13). If God dwells in each of us, then God cannot reject Godself in the person who has taken his or her own life.

If people imply that suicides are inferior Christians, I will give them an index card on which is printed a quote from Dietrich Bonhoeffer: "We must learn to regard people less in the light of what they do or omit to do, and more in the light of what they suffer."

And when I imagine what it must have been like for our son to stand before God in the depths of the woods with his gun in his hand, I ponder what his prayer must have been. I know he prayed either in his own words or simply by raising his heart to God in entreaty for the peace he could not go on breathing without.

The biblical prayer that seems to me to befit David's last moments on this earth comes from Queen Esther as she stood ready to lay down her life for her people: "Help me, who am alone and have no help but you, for I am taking my life in my hand" (Est C:14).

Our son, David Lorne Hutchinson, died at his own hand. And make no mistake, he is with God. God is not angry with him nor is God withholding an iota of love from him. The English mystic, Julian of Norwich, in her visions of Jesus, learned that "God's love and his wholeness cannot allow him to be angry." Anger and vengeance are "against the nature" of his strength, wisdom, and goodness.

My faith in God's compassionate love for our son is shored up by everyday epiphanies of David's presence to us and others who care deeply for him. These small revelations assure us that "We do not see them, but they see us. Their eyes, radiant with glory, are fixed upon our eyes full of tears. . .Though invisible to us, our dead are not absent" (Karl Rahner).

For instance: Four months after David's death, I was making chocolate cupcakes from scratch for two friends of his who were coming to dinner. I was half-way into the recipe when I discovered that my can of generic baking cocoa had about a tablespoon left in the bottom. Knowing that I had forgotten to buy a new can, I still began to paw through the baking ingredients as though I expected to find something.

There, behind the flour and baking powder, was an unopened can of first-class Nestle's baking cocoa that might as well have had my name on it. One of David's trademarks was always to buy the best brand of whatever was on his list. My lifelong habit is to buy the house brand.

Over the years, David and I often joked about his having to "run over to Burgess Market" to get whatever ingredient Mom was lacking in her latest baking project. He rarely complained or cast any aspersions on my absent-mindedness. Now, holding up the bright yellow costly can of Nestles, I said aloud, "Thanks, son. Hope you didn't have to go far to get it."

Another time I was in the O.R. suite of my ophthalmologist's office, waiting for the Valium to kick in before retinal surgery. Nondescript pop music had been playing in the background. I did not recognize any of the songs nor find them interesting. Suddenly a familiar melody broke through the banality. "I've been waiting for a girl like you to come into my life." It was a Foreigner song from the 1980s that David had practiced many times in his bedroom when he was in junior high. I loved that song. Now I took it as his way of letting me know that he was there, and all would be well.

Around 2 a.m. on the night after my surgery, I woke up and saw David standing in our bedroom doorway. He was larger than life and filled the entryway. His smile was beatific and he was wearing a beige Dockers shirt and workpants. I heard someone saying, "Well, look who's here." As I stared at him, he disappeared. It came to me later that the

Dockers might signify that he was doing God's work of caring for us and others.

I realize that what are revelations to me may be nothing more than coincidences or wishful thinking to others. But if we believe that our loved ones who have died remain a part of our lives, I think it would be selfish of them not to make their presence known in return. The three examples I have just given are quintessential David: humor, helpfulness, and sensitivity to other's needs.

Dave has been fortunate enough to dream more than once of our son. In one that mystified him, he was filling up the RV at a gas station near the Mojave Desert. He looked up idly and saw David walking by in the same direction we were heading.

"David!," he yelled.

Without breaking stride, David answered, "What do you want?"

"He wasn't rude or angry," Dave recalls. "It was sort of a business-like tone. I didn't know how to answer. So I called for you to come and see David and I woke myself up."

The scene reminded me of a gospel story in which Jesus is on the road to Jericho when two blind men call out to him. He stops and asks, "What do you want me to do for you?" (Mt 20:32). They tell him they want him to "open their eyes."

"If you have that dream again," I suggested, "Be sure to tell David you want him to open your eyes to why he left us. Maybe he will."

David's former wife Lisa has also had several dreams in which he appeared. "In one a little boy angel was breathing peace into him. David too was a young boy. They were both down on their hands and knees in a yoga 'child pose.' It was a very cool dream."

The yoga connection struck me as a revelation. Right after David's death, I had a vision of him with our friend Francis McGillicuddy who had died of cancer a few years ago. Francis and his wife Elaine once owned a yoga studio and were dedicated practitioners who loved to initi-ate others into this Eastern discipline. I "saw" David and Francis with their arms around each others' shoulders. They were grinning like lepre-chauns, looking delighted to be in each other's company.

When I told Elaine about the vision, she wrote, "These are myster-ies we know not of, and when we go into 'Death Valley' the veil is thin. That's one of the gifts of touching something so awe-ful."

During the last three weeks before David's death, I wrote out on an index card for him a scriptural or spiritual quote that might have meaning for him at this juncture in his life. I placed the card next to his coffee cup. He never mentioned them. But every morning he moved the day's card from one spot to another to signify that he had seen it.

I have no idea which ones spoke to him. I do not know if any of them seemed prescient to him, since he knew what he was about to do and I did not. However, I am certain that he did not ignore or totally reject them. David was a spiritual person who, like many alcoholics, used "spirits" to seek the Spirit who seemed to elude him.

On the first Sunday when I put out the scripture card for him, I also left a note about how his father needed him to check the truck tires and add air as needed. The next time I went to get a cup of coffee, there was a note from David for my spiritual instruction. It said, "Exodus 35:2: For six days work is to be done, but the seventh shall be your day of rest" and "Genesis 2:2: On the seventh day God had finished his work and rested." A smiley face appeared as David's signature.

When I jokingly asked him what translation of the Bible he was using, he quipped, "My own."

Among the quotes he must have taken to heart are these:

"Come to me, all you who are weary and find life burdensome, and I will refresh you" (Mt 11:28 NAB)

May [the Lord] grant you what is in your heart and fulfill your every plan. (Ps 20:5 NAB)

God indeed is my savior;
I am confident and unafraid. (Is 12:2 NAB)

It is possible (I hope it may be so) that God spoke to David in an intimate way through those hallowed words, and that David knew that he was being addressed in the most personal manner.

It is possible (I hope it may be so) that God called David home through those hallowed words, knowing that David was no longer capable of sustaining the burdens his bad choices, addictions, depressions and possible mental illness had thrust upon him.

It is possible (I hope it may be so) that although these hallowed words did not prevent David from leaving us, they did go with him into that dark night, assuring him that he was not alone.

It is possible (I hope it may be so) that David, whose second language was music, entered Paradise singing *What Wondrous Love Is This* to which the closing line is "And through eternity I'll sing on, I'll sing on."

In what seems an undeniable sign to me, on what would have been David's 50th birthday his friend and drummer Larry Ladrie wrote the following tribute on his Facebook page:

"David goes on singing in all our hearts."

CHAPTER 14

SUICIDE UNSHAMED

If you put shame in a Petri dish, it needs three things to grow: secrecy, silence, and judgment. If you put the same amount of shame in a Petri dish and douse it with empathy, it can't survive. The two most powerful words when we're in a struggle: me too.

Bréne Brown

"**S**uicide" has been coming out of the closet in recent headlines. It is still a dirty word. But it is uttered aloud more often. The news is both good and bad. It indicates that the suicide rate in this country is rising. But it also reveals a greater public willingness to look at why so many people are killing themselves, and why it has taken us so long as a society to do something about it.

As gay Americans are now winning approval for same-sex marriage, so those who have taken their own lives, those who have attempted it, and those who survive them will emerge from the dark valley of shame to which they have been consigned for too long by society and religion. When empathy replaces judgment, suicide will be "unshamed."

The self-inflicted death of Matthew Warren in April 2013 was widely reported. The 27-year old son of mega-church pastor Rick Warren had ordered an unregistered gun on the Internet. He returned home after going out to dinner with his parents and having what his father described as "a fun time." Then, in "a momentary wave of despair," he shot himself.

Despite their devastation at Matthew's death, the pastor and his wife Kay openly discussed the mental illness that had plagued their son. They revealed that Matthew had suffered from depression and suicidal thoughts for most of his life. A decade before he killed himself, Matthew had asked his father, "Dad, I know I'm going to heaven. Why can't I just die and end this pain?"

If our son David had felt free to speak as openly to us years ago, he too might have asked, "Dad, Mom, why can't I just die and end this pain?"

And if we had been educated about suicide, its causes and warning signs, might we have somehow been able to persuade him to get the help he needed?

We will never know. But we do know that we will do whatever we can to awaken others to the great tragedy of one troubled person killing himself or herself every 15 minutes in this country.

According to the Centers for Disease Control and Prevention, more people died of suicide (38,364) than of motor vehicle accidents (33,687) in 2010. The self-inflicted death rates are rising particularly among veterans, middle-aged adults, teens, and gay and lesbian people.

There are no accurate counts of suicides because of the stigma attached to those who take their own lives and those who survive them. The victims are blamed for their "sin" or "weakness." Their families are blamed for not preventing their loved one from killing himself or herself. They are shamed by the criminal investigation which the police are required to make into any suicide.

Guilt and shame have been so liberally heaped upon the heads of everyone involved in the suicide that the true cause of death is often hidden even from extended family members. At times those who know bury the knowledge deep inside and actually "forget" that it happened. Since our son's death, several friends have confided the following to us:

+ "I never knew that my grandfather killed himself until I overheard a dinner conversation in which the guest said to my father, 'So it looks like your father committed suicide, right?' And my father said, 'That's about it.' I had been told that he died of a stroke. They were too ashamed to tell me the truth and didn't want me to suffer any embarrassment at school."

+ "My husband's brother supposedly died of a heart attack. But we found out later that he actually turned a shotgun on himself. He had borrowed over $70,000 from my father-in-law and never paid it back. We only found out when my father-in-law died and the money that was supposed to be divided among the sons was missing. I felt terrible that my brother-in-law killed himself over money."

+ "I had completely blocked this out of my memory. But when someone else admitted that their relative killed himself, I heard myself saying "Oh!" It happened years ago and we never talk about it. My husband's cousin Bill was a very gregarious person who used to be a DJ on the radio. Then he went into business and he overextended himself. We were out of touch for quite awhile. Then, out of the blue, we heard that he had shot himself at an isolated camp somewhere."

+ Another friend brought to our attention the obituary for a fifteen-year old boy named Jesse Vedder Edwards-Borowicz who had killed himself in the family's Erie, PA home. Written by his mother, the obituary included these words: "Jesse was a member of Wayside Presbyterian Church . . .As a young gay man, Jesse found great support at his church and among his friends and family, and he looked forward hopefully to the day when there would be full equality for all."

In response to the obituary, Benedictine Sister Mary Lou Kownacki wrote of her deep sorrow over the cause of Jesse's self-inflicted death. She said she "wept for the sins of churches like my own who through their exclusion and cruel pronouncements help make life a hell for beautiful young people like Jesse."

I was filled with admiration for Alice Edwards, Jesse's mother, who openly declared his membership in the gay community. And I was ashamed of my own unwillingness to state in our son's obituary the cause of his death. I could come no closer than "died unexpectedly." For many of us, the stigma still holds sway.

Are we afraid that if we talk about suicide, we will have to face our own fears of death? Do we avoid the subject because we have a primal feeling that it might be "catching"?

Who or what might help us roll away the stone of humiliation and blame that blocks our empathy for those who die at their own hands? It has been estimated that a million Americans attempt to kill themselves every year. What can we do to alleviate this public health crisis?

In a book on the connection between the artistic temperament and manic-depressive illness, I found a saving insight. Kay Redfield Jamison, professor of psychiatry, writes: "The overwhelming majority of all . . .who commit suicide have been determined, through postmortem investigations, to have suffered from either bipolar manic-depression or unipolar depressive illness" (*Touched With Fire: Manic-Depressive Illness and the Artistic Temperament*, Simon & Schuster, NY 1993, p.16). These investigations are based on autobiography, biography, and medical records.

The author also points out that four related factors account for more than 80% of suicides among adolescents: bipolar illness, alcohol and/or drug abuse, lack of medical treatment, and availability of firearms (p. 41).

Bipolar illness refers to a wide range of mood disorders and temperaments. Symptoms run the gamut from hopelessness and impaired memory to suicidal thinking and self-blaming. Professor Jamison's book illustrates the connections between melancholy, madness, and creativity.

Although my need for the "Why?" of David's death may be driving me too far in this direction, I can accurately list the following bipolar symptoms which he displayed in the last few years of his life:

+ When he had "the flu" (undiagnosed), David reported seeing monsters above his bed and hearing them threaten him. Were these hallucinations generated by a fever or a psychosis?

+ When his father contradicted him about certain financial matters at the store, David began raving, shouting obscenities and abusive charges against Dave who was shocked by the unhinged attack. Was this emotional turbulence generated by alcohol or bipolar disease, or both?

+ When David and I were watching the news one evening, he became overly-excited about what he saw as the chicanery of certain politicians who opposed health care reform. He began talking irrationally, his words tumbling over one another. My attempts to defuse him were blocked by his loud rapid-fire monologue. Was this extreme intensity a sign of stress or mental illness?

+ When his various bands had finished playing for the night, his friends recall that David drank steadily while talking passionately about admired musicians like Paul Rodgers and Eric Clapton, Bob Dylan and John Lennon. He dominated the conversation until the others gave up and went to bed. Was this completely out of character behavior simply alcoholism or bipolar volatility?

He had mood swings, depressions, periodic inflated self-esteem. At times he worked fanatically on his music, burning himself out in the drive for "getting it right." He sometimes ran away from relationships, attempting to escape the burden of himself. However, most of the time he was "clinically normal."

If the majority of those who, like David, take their own lives are suffering from one or more mental illnesses, should they be judged or commiserated with? Lord Byron, himself a manic-depressive, wrote, "We did not make ourselves, and if the element of unhappiness abound more in the nature of one man than another, he is but the more entitled to our pity and our forebearance [*sic*]" (Jamison, p. 153).

The suicides among us, as well as their families, do not belong in the dark alleys of "secrecy, silence and judgment." They need our empathy, understanding, and assistance.

We need your willingness to walk in our shoes and say out loud those two most powerful words, "Me too." Either you or someone you know may be among the million who attempted suicide this past year. Someone you love may have succeeded in ending his or her life. Someone in your church or neighborhood may be reaching the end of his or her rope right now.

By learning how to recognize the signs of addictive behavior, we can help others to turn away from the death that seems to be their only option. We can show them that their lives are indeed worth living. We can remind them that "Suicide is a permanent solution to a temporary problem." For their families, we can promote more suicide grief support groups and take every opportunity to de-shame the taking of one's own life.

In my own state of Maine, which has the eleventh highest suicide rate in the country, a bill was recently passed to require educators to be trained in recognizing the signs that a young person may be considering suicide. As one supporter pointed out, the signs are often invisible to the person's loved ones. Parents and siblings need others in the community who can discern the would-be suicide's fatal intentions.

For those whose lives have never been darkened by the horror of suicide, there are good reasons to increase awareness about self-inflicted death. Suicide rates in the United States have risen sharply among the following groups: teens, gays (LGBTQ), veterans, Native Americans, and baby boomers. A sixth group, which overlaps all the others, is gun owners or those who have firearms available to them.

The New York Times reported in February 2013 that about 20,000 of the annual 30,000 deaths by firearms each year are suicides. A Florida State University criminology professor, Gary Kleck, observed that those who own guns "may be more apt to see the world as a hostile place, and blame themselves when things go wrong--the dark side of self-reliance." (Here again hindsight reveals how well our son fit this description.)

In an article aptly titled "All Hands on Deck: How We Can Help Someone Who's Suicidal," Dr. Lisa Firestone alerts us to the reality that our loved ones, when in a suicidal state, are heeding cruel inner voices that turn them against themselves. The voices persuade them that they are worthless and should not even be alive. They drive the afflicted person to be "self-critical, self-hating. . .self-destructive."

Among Dr. Firestone's suggestions for helping the suicidal person to turn away from death are the following: (1) Reach out to them to help them stand up to their destructive inner voices; (2) Help them remember what they value in life and what has given them joy in the past; (3) Help orient them toward the future by showing them how to "create meaning out of adversity," and (4) Take the time to be truly connected to the person and assure them of how much they matter to us.

(This article and many others on suicide and violence can be accessed on the website *psychalive.org*. See also our list of resources in the back of this book.)

Once we as a society care enough about each other to bury the stigma of suicide and become aware of the signs of its threatened presence, there will be fewer Davids, Seths and Sheilas lost by the wayside. There will be fewer families drenched in this valley of tears.

Together we pray, "Let it be."

CHAPTER 15

FINDING DAVID

*And I believe, with good evidence,
that there are no exceptions to
resurrection.*

Richard Rohr

When someone we love, deeply and through length of years, takes his or her own life, we "never get over it." Our mourning may become more discreet. Our unseemly hunger for the lost one's physical presence may be better hidden. However, our manner of navigating through this life has been permanently changed. We are forever seeking the one who is surely here yet visible only to the eyes of the heart.

Because we believe in resurrection, we know that David's death was not the end of the story. Not his. Not ours. After attending dying Hospice patients for many years, Kathleen Dowling Singh assures us that "the life and death of a human being is exquisitely calibrated to automatically produce union with Spirit at the end" (*The Grace in Dying*, p. 15). Those who bring about their own death are not exempted from this universal process.

Because we believe in resurrection, we know that David will ever be a part of our lives. There will never come a day when he ceases to be.

We will be seeking him in countless places, many of which we have yet to discover. But we begin with the familiar: in each other's blue eyes, in Dave's curly reddish-blond hair, in our above average height, in the faces of his daughters, in his music, and in the places where he kept company with us.

Beyond these people and places, I am seeking David in the lyrics of his favorite songs and sifting the evidence of his best-loved movies. Before his death, I never looked twice at these intimations of his inner life. Now I peer into them with the avidity of a cold case detective studying a DNA report. I want to know whatever they can tell me about our son.

For instance: why was a brilliant mind like David's so attracted to a character with an I.Q. of 75 whose naivete often made him look like an incurable simpleton? *Forrest Gump* is the story of an oddball who somehow finds his way into the most important events of American history from the 1950s through the 1980s. His sufferings always lead to better things, and he is guided solely by the homespun philosophy of his Mama.

Forrest's Mamaisms include:

+ "Life is like a box of chocolates. You never know what you're going to get."

+ "Stupid is as stupid does."

+ "You've got to put the past behind you before you can move on."

+ "Mama always said dying was a part of life. I sure wish it wasn't."

My guess is that these simple truisms appealed to David whose own mind was so laden with complicated theories about the meaning of life, how to measure up to its demands, and how to achieve one's dreams. Forrest, an intellectual underdog, succeeded at whatever he did. Our son must have pined for such an unattainable happiness.

I wonder if David also identified with Forrest's childhood friend, Jenny, a world-weary and addictive personality, who took years to recognize how much she loved the childlike Forrest. One of David's oft-quoted lines from the movie is Jenny's prayer: "Dear God, make me a bird so I can fly far, far, far away from here.",

I wonder too what David made of the movie's mysterious feather floating above Forrest's head at the beginning and end of his story. To me, it suggested the mystic Hildegard of Bingen referring to herself as "a feather on the breath of God." She felt held aloft by a loving God. Forrest Gump lived as one favored by a benevolent Deity. Did David?

Another favorite was the 1989 movie *Parenthood* in which several generations of one family are dealing with the familiar crises of divorce, drug abuse, parental expectations, stressful relationships, and being an outsider in society and/or the family. Did David identify with the addicted son (Tom Hulce) or the high-anxiety get-everything-right son (Steve Martin). I suspect it was the latter.

A third favorite was *The Blues Brothers* with the oft-repeated Jake and Elwood line, "We're on a mission from God." These two wacky good-hearted musicians who are out to save a Catholic orphanage must have appealed to David's own commitment to doing benefit gigs for nonprofit groups and worthy causes. Did this movie validate for him that even rock musicians of wild reputation could be called upon to get things done for God?

Along with these three comedies, two dramas stood near the top of David's see-again list. He loved *Lost in Translation* and *A Beautiful Mind*. The first is about a middle-aged actor who is in Tokyo to make a mindless whiskey commercial. His marriage isn't working; his career is unsatisfying. He meets a young woman and a friendship builds between them. The nature of their relationship remains mysterious, but they are both enriched by it

The second tells the story of John Forbes Nash, Jr., the mathematical genius who developed a game theory that eventually won him a Nobel Prize. Nash is a misfit who suffers from paranoid schizophrenia. He has trouble relating to others and is scarred by his second grade teacher's observation that he had "two helpings of brain but only one of heart." His hallucinations and inability to discern what is real from what is not nearly ruin his marriage. Once his madness has been medically treated, his genius is reined in.

In both stories, David must have found common ground with mid-life men whose creativity and intellect could not shield them from the dark side of life. Their troubled marriages and loneliness echoed his own.

Similar themes arise in the music David most admired. "Shooting Star," by Paul Rodgers of Bad Company, recounts the sad tale of Johnny, a young guitar player who runs off with a rock n' roll band to make his fortune. His Mama asks, "Don't you know that you are a shooting star?" She warns him that the world's acclaim will not last forever. When her prophecy comes true, Johnny kills himself with whiskey and sleeping pills. (Rogers says he wrote this song as a warning to his fellow musicians.)

Three other favored songs whose prescient lyrics escaped me before David's death are "Basket Case" by Green Day's Billie Joe Armstrong who suffered from a panic disorder ("My mind plays tricks on me" and "Am I just paranoid?"); "Behind Blue Eyes" by The Who's Pete Townshend ("No one knows what it's like/To be the bad man/To be the sad man/Behind blue eyes."); "Creep" by Radiohead in which the singer is a misfit who insists "I don't belong here/I don't belong here."

In time, I will remember too all the good time, foot stomping, heart raising, hope giving songs David played and sang at countless celebrations where people gathered together for a wedding reception, an anniversary or graduation party, a block party, a fair, a concert, or just a Saturday night on the town.

His music created community and he knew how to be a celebrant. There was more, much more, to it than everyone having a few beers and singing off-key with the band.

One memorable example was the night years ago when Bruce and the Crew Cuts as a brand new band had a gig at the Lone Star in Fort Kent. When a rowdy group of Harley bikers arrived, both the band and the rest of us in the audience got a bit nervous. We all worried about what these "outsiders" might do. If the guitar players hadn't been wearing their terry cloth tennis wristbands to catch the sweat, their Fender strings would have rusted in no time.

After listening to a song or two without incident, one of the bikers called out, "Play 'That'll Be the Day'!"

He didn't have to say "Please." The band knew just about every song Buddy Holly ever wrote. David had taught them the music and the lyrics. Now all they had to do was play it well enough to keep the Harley boys happy.

At the opening chords, the bikers in black shoved back their chairs and grabbed every unattended woman in the club. When they ran out of women, they grabbed each other, roared along with David ("Well, that'll be the day when you say goodbye"), clomped their biker boots, and rocked their hearts out.

When it was over, two of the satisfied customers went up to the stage and stuffed five dollar bills into David's sweaty hand. "What a relief," he later told me. "I was afraid they might throw pizza or beer at us."

In later years, when David and Dennis Boyd teamed up as an acoustic duo, they played to quieter crowds in smaller venues. Dennis' wife Janet recalls their gigs at the Oak Tavern in Rochester, NH, where the music "was almost magical." She recalls, "We all sat in amazement listening to 'John' [Lennon] and 'Paul' [McCartney] who were there with us through David and Dennis' beautiful voices. Now that David is gone, a piece of Dennis' musical soul is forever lost."

That's our son. His music, originals and cover tunes, made people happy, urged them to forget their troubles, hauled them out of their chairs and onto the dance floor, made them glad to be alive, sorry when it was over.

At lunch one day my friend Marge Adams told a story recorded by the anthropologist

Loren Eiseley. It was called *The Judgment of the Birds*. Marge summarized it this way:

"A huge raven descended on a sparrows' nest and grabbed a baby bird. The parents squawked and cried but the raven flew off with the chick. Then lots of other little birds who heard the parents' grieving came and circled around the nest. At first they cried out with the parents against the raven. But gradually, their songs changed to a more joyous sound. It was like they knew that death does not have the last word."

When I found this story in *The iDeal Reader* (McGraw Hill, 2001), I delighted in Eiseley's closing sentence: "In simple truth, they had forgotten the raven, for they were the singers of life, and not of death."

Likewise, the black raven of David's suicide can, in time, recede into the forest where dim memories retire from public view. And he will be remembered as a singer of life, not death.

EPILOGUE

*The living owe it to those who can no
longer speak to tell their story for them.*

--Czeslaw Milosz

We can't go home again to that home where our son slept downstairs, sat at the Sunday dinner table, took long showers in the guest bathroom, rode the red lawnmower in long rows across the back yard, parked his jaunty yellow Jeep in front of the second garage door, and lifted our spirits every time he walked through the door.

That home no longer exists, although the house it occupied still stands. A couple called Dave and Gloria live here. But Mom and Dad have vanished into the fog-shrouded past. Dave has planted trees (mountain ash for David, weeping cherry for us) and landscaped with stonework to alter the painful familiarity of the place.

Across the road, where the hackmatacks and pines jostle each other for growing space, a new home has risen on a cement foundation laid during the sixth month after David's death. Theoretically, we prefer the unadulterated forest. But whatever changes the landscape aids our recovery from grief. We welcome the intrusion on our son's mossy deathbed.

We still light the vigil candle from David's memorial every afternoon at 3 p.m. We pour two glasses of wine (sangria for me, white zin for him) and raise our glasses to David and to the new life we are attempting to live. This simple ritual has comforted us from the start. My favorite toast is one Dave offered in the early days after David's death: "Here's to the healing of broken hearts!"

I know that our son's bodily presence is gone. But his spirit, his essence, his Davidness will be with us always.

We will go on evading terminal sadness by inviting friends over for dinner, hosting our granddaughters a few times a year, touring national parks to be awed by wilderness and consoled by wildlife, collecting shells along Florida's beaches and rocks in Arizona's mountains, gathering with spiritual book groups, seeking wisdom in scripture and inspired movies, supporting causes that matter to us with the emphasis on suicide prevention and comforting the survivors, praying for peace within and without.

We will be grateful all over again for a truth my friend Barbara pointed out in her eulogy: "David loved his parents deeply. He never told me that. I saw it in his life."

We will imagine how David, in some mysterious way, is both with us and gone to that promised "land more kind than home" (Thomas Wolfe). When our courage is high, we will listen again to *Any Day Now*, knowing that our son's soul is singing still.

In time, we will move beyond damage done to make peace with the sun.

We will. We surely will.

Any day now.

RESOURCES FOR CARING READERS:

Those Grieving a Suicide,
Those Who Have Attempted a Self-Inflicted Death,
Those Intending to End Their Lives,
Those Who Recognize Their Call to Help Prevent Suicide.

LIST A

TEN SIGNS THAT A PERSON MAY BE CONSIDERING SUICIDE

1. He is depressed or moody for an extended period.
2. She is disinterested in her usual activities and avoids her friends.
3. He has suffered a major loss or broken relationship.
4. She acts recklessly in driving, spending money, or in risky relationships.
5. He loses interest in food.
6. She repeatedly talks about death.
7. He organizes and gives away many of his belongings.
8. She becomes inexplicably calm and contented after being depressed.
9. He feels he is a failure and is despairing about the future.
10. She shows interest in acquiring firearms, sleeping pills, or other means of completing suicide.

LIST B

TEN THINGS YOU CAN DO TO HELP THE WOULD-BE SUICIDE

1. Ask if he or she has considered suicide, and pay close attention to the response.
2. Take any statements about self-destruction seriously.
3. Encourage him to express feelings openly. Listen respectfully.
4. Accept and do not judge whatever feelings are voiced.
5. Avoid preaching against suicide or arousing the person's defensiveness.
6. Be kind and direct. Don't beat around the bush.
7. Empathize with the person by imagining yourself in his or her shoes.
8. Keep an open mind on the possibility that this threat may be acted upon.
9. Help the person to see that he or she has a future and cause for hope.
10. Seek professional help and offer to stand by the person in need.

LIST C

TEN WAYS TO BE PART OF THE SUICIDE SOLUTION

1. Help to erase the stigma of suicide by talking openly about any experience, direct or indirect, that you may have had with suicide.
2. Compile and share information on finding qualified suicide counselors and local mental health resources.
3. Support programs and organizations that treat alcohol and drug addiction.
4. Encourage your local newspaper(s), radio or TV station(s) to publicize suicide as a major public health issue and show how it affects families and communities.
5. Become a member or supporter of the American Foundation for Suicide Prevention (www.afsp.org). This organization offers many ways to get involved, including the Out of Darkness Walks to prevent suicide. AFSP exists in all 50 states.
6. Join Families for Depression Awareness (www.familyaware.org) to participate in their goals of eliminating suicide stigma, uniting families, recognizing and dealing with depression.
7. Join Heartbeat to participate in their Grief Support Following Suicide program (www.heartbeatsurvivorsaftersicide.org). Look for similar

support groups associated with local medical centers and funeral homes.

8. Become a member of the Suicide Prevention Action Network USA (capwiz.com/spanusa/home). Among their activities is the writing of advocacy letters to media and government leaders to raise public awareness of this issue.

9. Organize a book group to explore how humanity's view of suicide has developed over the ages. Discover some of the most persuasive arguments against taking one's own life by reading Jennifer Michael Hecht's *Stay: A History of Suicide and the Philosophies Against It* (Yale University, 2013).

10. Organize at your church or among your friends a Suicide Alert Prayer Team which can be called by families in need of spiritual support when a loved one is threatening suicide or attempted or succeeded in it. Or use social networking to provide the same service.

LIST D

TEN SONGS TO COMFORT THE GRIEVING

1. *Everybody Hurts* (R.E.M.) (Michael Stipe, Mike Mills, Peter Buck, Bill Berry)
2. *All I Ask of You* (Weston Priory) (Gregory Norbet)
3. *Let It Be* (The Beatles) (John Lennon, Paul McCartney)
4. *Be Not Afraid* (St. Louis Jesuits) (Bob Dufford)
5. *Tears in Heaven* (Eric Clapton)
6. *My Heart Will Go On* (Celine Dion) (Will Jennings and James Horner)
7. *Fire and Rain* (James Taylor)
8. *Shepherd Me, O God (Psalm 23)* (Marty Haugen)
9. *Brighter Side* (OPM) (Sabelle Breer, Andrew Fromm, David Greenberg, Matthew Meschery, John Chrles Edney, Geoffrey H. Turney)
10. *Abide With Me* (Henry F. Lyte)

LIST E

TEN POEMS TO EASE THE PAIN

1. *The Land of Beginning Again* (Louisa Fletcher)
2. *Any Morning (William Stafford)*
3. *The Summer Day* (Mary Oliver)
4. *A Prayer in the Prospect of Death* (Robert Burns)
5. *No Hemlock Rock (don't kill yourself)* (Jennifer Michael Hecht)
6. *Dirge Without Music* (Edna St. Vincent Millay)
7. *Let Evening Come* (Jane Kenyon)
8. *My Own Heart* (Gerard Manley Hopkins)
9. *Afraid! Of Whom Am I Afraid?* (Emily Dickinson)
10. *A Short Testament* (Anne Porter)

LIST F

TEN BOOKS TO INFORM AND INSPIRE

1. Collins, Judy. *Sanity & Grace: A Journey of* Suicide, *Survival and Strength.* New York: Penguin, 2003.
2. Fine, Carla. *No Time to Say Goodbye: Surviving the Suicide of a Loved One.* New York: Broadway Books, 2000.
3. Cobain, Beverly and Jean Larch. *Dying to Be Free: A Healing Guide for Families After a Suicide.* Center City, MN: Hazelden, 2006.
4. Hsu, Albert. *Grieving a Suicide: A Loved One's Search for Comfort, Answers & Hope.* IVP Books, 2002.
5. Jamison, Kay Redfield. *Touched with Fire: Manic-Depressive Illness and the Artistic Temperament.* New York: Simon & Schuster, 1993.
6. Lewis, C. S. *A Grief Observed.* Faber Paperbacks, 2012.
7. Lukas, Christopher and Henry M. Seiden. *Silent Grief: Living in the Wake of Suicide.* Jessica Kingsley Publishers, 1998.
8. Singh, Kathleen Dowling. *The Grace in Dying: A Message of Hope, Comfort and Spiritual Transformation.* San Francisco: Harper, 2000.
9. Wickersham, Joan. *The Suicide Index: Putting My Father's Death in Order.* Boston: Houghton Mifflin Harcourt, 2008.
10. Wolfelt, Alan D. *The Wilderness of Suicide Grief: Finding Your Way.* Companion Press, 2010.

LIST G

TEN MOVIES TO DEEPEN LOVE FOR LIFE

1. *To the Wonder* (Terrence Malick) A visual hymn of praise to sacred and romantic love, accompanied by a gorgeous soundtrack of classical music.
2. *Avatar* (James Cameron) Imaginative story set in 2154 on planet Pandora, where ecological and anti-war themes are played out.
3. *Heaven is for Real* (Sue Baden-Powell) A true story of four-year old Colton Burpo's near death experience and his attempts to persuade his father that he has been to heaven.
4. *Like Water for Chocolate* (Alfonso Arau) A romantic fable from Mexico in which young lovers are finally united after overcoming numerous obstacles. Love and good food take center stage.
5. *Billy Elliot* (Stephen Daldry) A young boy in a British coal mining town discovers that he has a talent for ballet. His coal miner father and brother finally come around, and Billy Elliot fulfills his dream. Exuberant dancing arouses joy in being alive.
6. *It's a Wonderful Life* (Frank Capra) A small town banker facing ruin is helped by an angel to see what a difference he has made to his family and community. He decides against taking his own life.

7. *Life of Pi* (Ang Lee) A boy from India and a Bengal tiger form a strong bond while spending 227 days on a raft at sea after a shipwreck. Beautiful production with endearing characters.

8. *Life is Beautiful* (Roberto Benigni) An Italian Jewish shop keeper spins a fantasy to protect his small son in a Nazi concentration camp. He concocts a fake contest in which a German tank is the prize. Guido gives his life for his son.

9. *The Color Purple* (Steven Speilberg) Celie, a poor black woman in the rural South, learns how to overcome an abusive husband, love herself, and enter into the joy of life. Offers a strong incentive not to give up on life during times of trial.

10. *A River Runs Through It* (Robert Redford) Beautiful film celebrating the art of fly fishing as a metaphor for life. Father and two sons devoted to each other and to joy of fishing well. Younger son lives recklessly and throws his life away.

LIST H

TEN SCRIPTURAL MESSAGES OF HOPE IN HARD TIMES

1. The Book of Job (See especially Chapters 40, 42 with the reassuring final verse, after all of Job's horrendous suffering, he died "old and full of years.)
2. Psalm 8 (See especially verses 5-7 on the dignity of humanity.)
3. Psalm 23 (The entire psalm verifies the Lord's surpassing love for each of us.)
4. Psalm 56 (See especially verse 9 on our tears and wanderings.)
5. Psalm 139 (The entire psalm verifies how God intimately knows and cherishes us.)
6. Matthew 10:28-33 (Jesus assures us of our great worth.)
7. Luke 15:1-32 (Three parables about finding the lost.)
8. John 16:20-22 (Grief is turned into joy.)
9. 2 Corinthians 4:16-18 (We do not lose heart.)
10. Jeremiah 29:11-14 (God's plan for good for you.)

LIST I

THE AUTHOR'S ADVICE FROM
HARD EXPERIENCE

1. Pray, whether you believe or not.
2. Tell your sorrow. Don't bury it.
3. Share your lost loved one's story.
4. Vent your anger about the injustice of suicide. (If you don't have any anger, think again.)
5. Interview your loved one's friends, relatives, acquaintances to discover who he [she] was to them.
6. Gather photos from throughout your loved one's life. Reflect on what the camera reveals about him [her].
7. List your loved one's favorite books, movies and music to find clues about his [her] inner life.
8. On paper or film, count the ways in which you love the one you have lost and tell him [her] why.
9. Join or form a suicide survivors support group to gain and give comfort and guidance.
10. Pray, whether you believe or not. Perhaps in time you will.

A PRAYER FOR THOSE WHO ARE DECIDING NOT TO GO ON

Giver of Life, whose name is Love, look with mercy on your lost ones who are weighing their lives, judging them lacking. Break up the ice of their despair, secure them against harsh gusts of fear, heal their hopelessness. Still the sour voices insinuating failure. Wrap them in arms mightier than death. Will them to see that they are beyond price. Convince them that we care.

Amen.

Let it be.

18193045R00082